NEW WRITING / BOOK

THE RE,

No. 48 WINTER 2012

Published by The Reader Organisation

the reader
organisation

EDITOR | Philip Davis

DEPUTY EDITOR | Sarah Coley
CO-EDITORS | Lizzie Cain
Maura Kennedy
Angela Macmillan
Eleanor McCann
Brian Nellist

ADDRESS | The Reader Magazine
The Reader Organisation
The Friary Centre
Bute Street
Liverpool
L5 3LA

EMAIL | magazine@thereader.org.uk
WEBSITE | www.thereader.org.uk
BLOG | www.thereaderonline.co.uk

DISTRIBUTION | See p. 128
COVER IMAGE | Michael Troy, Artist and Illustrator, 'Aussie Outback', Mixed Media

ISBN 978-0-9567862-7-2

SUBMISSIONS

The Reader genuinely welcomes submissions of poetry, fiction, essays, readings and thought. We publish professional writers and absolute beginners. Send your manuscript with SAE please to:

The Reader Organisation, The Friary Centre, Bute Street, Liverpool, L5 3LA

Printed and bound in the European Union by Bell and Bain Ltd, Glasgow

NEWS AND EVENTS

CROESO! WALES WELCOMES THE READER ORGANISATION

The Reader Organisation has received over £200,000 from Big Lottery Wales for a three-year project to set up Get Into Reading groups and provide training opportunities in North Wales. Over 30 groups will reach some 480 people in an area where poor literacy skills and social isolation are higher than average. This, the first Get Into Reading project in Wales, will see our first bilingual groups with literature read aloud in English and Welsh.

WELLBEING PARTNERSHIP EXPANDS ACROSS NORTH WEST

The North West Strategic Health Authority has commissioned The Reader Organisation to deliver Get Into Reading in every Mental Health Trust in the North West of England. In collaboration with NHS Cheshire and Warrington and Wigan PCT Cluster, 5 new Project Workers will deliver 24 sustainable groups and provide in-house training so NHS staff will be able to take over group facilitation. The groups will take place in community settings through to secure units, improving wellbeing across the region.

DANNY BOYLE VISITS HOPE READERS

Oscar-winning director Danny Boyle thrilled staff and students at Liverpool Hope University's Faculty of Education in October when he visited to deliver a special lecture with Frank Cottrell Boyce as part of The Reader Organisation's Hope Readers Project. The pair discussed the books and writers who have inspired their work, particularly their collaboration on the London 2012 Olympic Opening Ceremony. The Hope Readers Project aims to nurture a culture of reading for pleasure amongst the future teachers, so they can share their enthusiasm with the next generation. [See Jane's article on page 86 for more on the visit.]

GUARDIAN CHILDREN'S FICTION PRIZE

The Unforgotten Coat, written by Frank Cottrell Boyce 'as a gift' for The Reader Organisation, has won the *Guardian* Children's Fiction Prize. Praised by the judges for containing a 'very profound message dressed up in a magical, original, humorous story'. The book was inspired by a Mongolian girl whom Frank met at a local primary school, whose deportation haunted him and whose forgotten coat worried her classmates.

CONTENTS

JANE DAVIS
TRYING ON A HAT

EDITORIAL

MOODY

Philip Davis

I n 'Ask the Reader' this time Brian Nellist deals with the hullabaloo over the bicentenary of Dickens's birth. But we must come clean. *The Reader* itself was invited to Buckingham Palace a few months ago to celebrate the event – and accepted on your behalf.

Your reporter gloomily prepared himself psychically and sartorially to meet the good and the great. Would it be Melvyn, or Antonia, or . . . The first person to whom I was introduced turned out to be none other than the great Lord Bard of Barnsley, otherwise our own Ian McMillan. 'What are you doing here?' is what I heard us both saying at about the same time. The equivalent in its way to meeting a friend, in surprise, in the doctor's waiting room and enquiring after said friend's health (though this has happened to me so often of late that I have tutored myself into saying 'How do you *find* yourself?' instead).

I then did not so much meet the Ruth Jones of *Gavin and Stacey*, as fall against her. Graciously (there is no other adverb in the Palace) she apologised as though on my behalf. After that, among the people I did not then assault, insult or otherwise encounter were Simon Callow, Helena Bonham Carter (though my wife did ask a lady-in-waiting whether she knew if the Queen had enjoyed HBC's portrayal of her mother in *The King's Speech*), Patsy Kensit, Trevor Nunn, and Griff Rhys-Jones. We all formed a line to be introduced to the Queen and the Duke of Edinburgh. Reading the description on my name-badge, the Duke said to me with great enthusiasm, 'Liverpool!' And I said, 'Yes, indeed' with what I hoped was equal gusto, and then we were moved on towards the drinks and canapés.

By then, feeling a little shyly awkward, I had retreated to one side of the room to examine – carefully after the Ruth Jones encounter – a Canaletto. There was a woman just along from me doing the same and we exchanged appreciative noises until, still honing my questioning-style, I asked her what brought her to this gathering. She said: Who, not what. She was accompanying someone. I asked her who; and she said, 'Ron Moody'.

Ron Moody, some of you in *The Reader*'s demographic may warmly recall, played a magnificent Fagin in the film version of Lionel Bart's musical *Oliver!* back in 1986. I remember it was the first time I had ever gone to the cinema alone but I never felt alone throughout. This was a man of electrical talent: I felt it going right through me as I watched. He was so good that, later, my family feigned to believe he was a distant cousin.

So I said to the woman, in the relief of unforced delight, 'I *love* Ron Moody.' And she replied, 'So do I. I'm married to him.' 'I wish I was,' I said (which made my wife, nearby, offer me what in our house we somewhat misleadingly call a funny look), and I asked to meet him.

'I've always wanted to be you,' I told him. He was an old man now, sitting down to one side, and I thought of my dad who at ceremonies and celebrations would often take himself off to the oldest man in the house and sit by him. Ron Moody stared at my name-badge. 'And I,' he said drily, 'have always wanted to be a professor.' We talked about writing – he had published an autobiography in 2010 and wrote every day – and about the merit of academic tenure as compared to rapturous applause and charismatic fame. Then his wife said that their daughter would love it if we could get her the autograph of the film-maker Tim Burton, standing just a few feet away; but she didn't think it was right to ask. Then my wife said that I was so insensitive that I wouldn't mind asking him. Which I did, with a success that justified my reputation. By then I had plucked up so much courage as to ask for Ron Moody's own autograph, for me and various members of my family, and, as we left down the Mall, was feeling a sort of dangerously social exuberance.

In 2013 I am planning to be more expansive, with availability for weddings, funerals, Bar Mitzvahs, parties and celebrations, and even (despite the warnings of my friend Howard Jacobson in *Zoo Time*) literary festivals. Please send all such invitations to the address at the front of the magazine, indicating style of dress and mood preference.

A happy Christmas (despite what my other friend Clive Sinclair offers in this issue) and a very good New Year to all our readers.

EDITOR'S PICKS

Now the Centre is one year old, **Philip Davis** sets out his manifesto for the pioneering work carried out by the **Centre for Research into Reading, Information and Linguistic Systems**.

In fiction we have an excerpt from **Howard Jacobson**'s new novel 'Zoo Time', which narrates a painful meeting; **Clive Sinclair**'s 'A Bad Lot' is the rummest Christmas story you are likely to find this (or any) year.

Brian Turner writes powerfully on 'Phantom Noise' for Poet on His Work. And there is fine new poetry from **Andrew McNeillie**, **Chris Hardy**, **Emma Curran**, **Melissa Lee-Houghton** and **Sarah Lindon**.

Iona Heath (recent President of the Royal College of GPs) examines the relationship between books and medical practice in her wide-ranging conversation with Susan Charteris.

Angela Macmillan of 'Buck's Quiz' and 'Books About...' has a new book in time for Christmas, *A Little, Aloud for Children* (David Fickling Books, £9.99). Visit our website www.thereader.org.uk to get it for a mere £5.99 + p&p. **Brian Nellist**, guiding force for the magazine, has a new poetry anthology *Minted* also available from The Reader Organisation for £6.00 (see p. 68 for further details).

FACE TO FACE

MEET THE POET

ANDREW
McNEILLIE
on p.25

What is your ideal New Year?
The Chinese one.

A book for Christmas?
Dear Grieve: Letters to Hugh MacDiarmid edited by
John Manson

What do you hope to be given this year?
Good fortune for the next.

New Year's resolution?
To go to Sheltand and Whalsay in the Spring.

What I hope to get this Christmas

CHRIS
HARDY
on p.39

On Poetry by Glyn Maxwell – clever and
provocative writing about poetry, and what
makes it a poem not prose.

ZZ Top's new album *La Futura*, their first in
8 years, a steamy swamp of thick guitar and
Billy Gibbons throat-tearing voice. ZZ Top
have propelled LiTTLe MACHiNe www.little-
machine.com up and down the motorways
as we play at Literature Festivals.

Artemis Cooper's biography of Patrick Leigh
Fermour – a brave, honourable, Homeric life.

Is it hard to pick a Christmas gift for a poet?

Picking a gift for a poet couldn't be easier – we always need paper and we always need pens! The organic feeling of paper under my palm and a biro in my grip are an important part of writing for me. A poet's materials are so simple, but quite person-specific. If you're trying to pick a gift for a poet, find out what they write with. Bundle these essential supplies together for a perfect, personal, poetic gift.

EMMA CURRAN
on p.52

MELISSA LEE-HOUGHTON
on p.92

Favourite place in the world?

There's no sunset like the sunset you see in your own hometown, wandering down familiar streets where kids are playing at sword fights with sticks in fields and people are waving goodnight to one another. I love my hometown because I love familiarity. Many people think 'familiarity' is a dirty word but I listen to the same songs, walk familiar routes; it's a kind of meditation. I think this small town is glorious, when the sun sets over the rows of stone terraces, or when cherry blossom in the park swishes about my feet.

What I hope to get this Christmas

You are taking a risk if you buy a poet a book for Christmas, I'd say. A queue of books is already awaiting attention, each auditioning regularly for its moment to be read. A book token will certainly not go to waste. But if piles of books are already threatening to crowd the poet out of her home, maybe you'd prefer not to implicate yourself in the situation. Personally, I'm hoping for a proper Reading Light this Christmas. It may sound terribly sensible, but just picture it in the midst of obsession.

SARAH LINDON
on p.106

BRIAN TURNER

© Kim Buchheit

THE POET ON HIS WORK

ON WRITING 'PHANTOM NOISE'

Brian Turner

Phantom Noise

There is this ringing hum this
bullet-borne language ringing
shell-fall and static this late-night
ringing of threadwork and carpet ringing
hiss and steam this wing-beat
of rotors and tanks broken
bodies ringing in steel humming these
voices of dust these years ringing
rifles in Babylon rifles in Sumer
ringing these children their gravestones
and candy their limbs gone missing their
static-borne television their ringing
this eardrum this rifled symphonic this
ringing of midnight in gunpowder and oil this
brake pad gone useless this muzzle-flash singing this
threading of bullets in muscle and bone this ringing
hum this ringing hum this
ringing

'Phantom Noise' is taken from *Phantom Noise* (Bloodaxe Books, 2010) and reproduced here with the kind permission of the author and Bloodaxe Books

n the summer of 2008, the Lannan Foundation offered an amazing gift: *Solitude*. They provided a long stretch of time for me to work in a meditative space on the outskirts of Marfa, Texas (where several houses are dedicated to a writer-in-residency program). It's high desert country. West Texas border country. An unforgiving landscape made of a hard soil given creosote and mesquite. To picture the area, imagine the backdrops in *Giant, There Will Be Blood*, and *No Country for Old Men* – all three of these films shot footage in and around Marfa. In that desert country, as in most deserts, the landscape refuses to be ignored. It is a central character.

And it's where I went to invoke the ghosts. To listen to the past. To better understand how we live our lives as creatures of multiple time zones, where the past and the present and the future commingle – and how this dynamic plays out in my own life.

On most nights of the residency, I'd stay awake until about an hour or so after dawn and then sleep in until shortly after noon. It was the monsoon season. (A lofty word in a desert setting, *monsoon*, but there was a good deal of truth in its application.) I enjoyed standing out on the wooden porch to listen to the pelting rain of the afternoon deluge. The cloudbursts had a clockwork precision to them, as if the rain were on a timer set to strike each day at half past three. After dinner and the dishes, after the sun sank on the western horizon, I'd pick up my pen to write while the night's insects lifted their instruments in numbers too vast to comprehend.

I was struggling with the collection of poems that would become *Phantom Noise*. The manuscript worked under a different title at the time – *Talk the Guns*. Within the seclusion of the residency and those long nights listening to Coltrane and Jolie Holland and Philip Glass, I gave myself completely to the obsessive drive within me. I'd set the CD player on repeat until the music formed a wallpaper of sound around me.

Some nights I paced the room, back and forth, over and over – walking with the lines forming in my head, walking with the poems as they rose up into the world, attuning my body to the rhythm of the verse. Pacing, pacing. A kind of circling within. And night after night, verse by verse, I knew there was something I still wasn't getting at, something the verses had yet to reveal. That's probably not the right way to phrase it. It was as if my body knew that there was a very physical experience in language available to me, possibly, if I kept searching for it.

I eventually wrote the title poem to the collection ('Phantom Noise') while there in Marfa. The poem is connected to my own hearing loss and function due to military service and combat, but, as is often the case, the well runs deeper than the water we find at the surface. In other words, the term *phantom noise* refers to a medical condition, and the poem is partly derived from this, but the world of the poem – for me – evokes issues of PTSD, the echoes of trauma, the humming of the world within our heads, the ever cycling multiplicity of moments we each carry within, and more. It evokes the broken, fragmented landscape of war carried within the human frame. Ironically, as I talk about the poem, I find myself circling around it again. I am in the wider field where the poem has rooted itself. I am in the landscape of the book it is printed in.

Maybe I should circle it again, because I don't think we're anywhere closer to where this poem began, or how it came to exist on the page and in the air.

The *air*. That's the right word. It is the air that carries the water. It brings the deluge. It fills the well and provides for its depth. And, like rain, poems are carried by the air we breathe. They are made of the breath we give them.

The poem, 'Phantom Noise,' is a perfect example of this point. I was thinking of the gaps between things, memory and history's erasures, the spaces, the caesuras in life, and how they create a kind of rest note in the overall music of our lives. In a musical score, rest notes don't necessarily mark a space which is devoid of music; they mark a space in which rhythm exists, though it has become internalized and stripped of its tonality.

It's the same as when I drink coffee and talk to a friend at the local Costa coffee shop in Manchester. When I sometimes fall silent, an observant friend might recognize that my mind has drifted off to another space: Iraq, 2004. On the outside, I'm like a musical rest note. Inside, however…

At one point during my time in Texas, I listened to the poet Ross Gay recite his poem (available on www.fishousepoems.org), 'Cousin Drowses on the Flight to Kuwait.' A phenomenal poem. I felt an immediate connection to the poem and an affinity for its landscape. It was as if I'd discovered a poem that my own work had already been in conversation with for years. His use of rhythm within the caesura is what really piqued my ear and kept me pacing the room as I listened for my own poem.

Much of contemporary free verse leans on the downbeat of the phrase, linking phrase by phrase, one after another, to create momentum and energy within the larger construction of the poem. What I enjoyed most in 'Cousin Drowses on the Flight to Kuwait' was how the poem relies on the upbeat (the '*and* one *and* two *and*' from the musician's tool-kit). The words on the upbeat in Ross Gay's poem have a slight hover, or holding pause, too, which creates tension, expectation, curiosity, and rhythmic pull. The combination of caesura with the lift of language into the rhythmic pull of that upbeat encouraged and inspired me as I paced the room, repeating the phrase 'There is this ringing hum this…' over and over. I didn't know what would come next. But the poem's beat word, *this*, began to rise out of silence, out of that ringing space in the mind's landscape, to give voice to an experience which would otherwise have remained internalized, fuming. 'Phantom Noise' found its way into the world by relying on the music we carry in our breath and in our bodies, and by trusting in the idea that music can lead to the construction of an experience.

FICTION

Howard Jacobson

That last lunch I had with him, in a restaurant the size of a matchbox, was our first for more than two years. But for his rubbish wardrobe – British Home Stores chinos of the sort wives buy for husbands and on which he'd wiped his hands of hope a thousand times too often, and some sort of trekking jacket found in one of those safari shops at the Eros end of Piccadilly – I wouldn't have recognised him. He had lost half his teeth and all his hair. Never a talkative man even when times were good and the Pauillac flowed, he sat slumped over his food, a barely touched glass of house wine in front of him, not eating his beetroot salad, his elbows digging into the diners on either side of him, revolving his head violently as though wanting to shake out more teeth. 'Mmm,' he said, whenever our eyes or knees met. Not knowing what else to do, I began ripping at my fingernails under the table.

There are 'mmms' which denote quiet acceptance of the state of things, the slow workings of reflection, or simply embarrassment. Merton's 'mmms' were none of these. Merton's 'mmms' indicated the futility of speech.

For which reason they were infectious. 'Mmm,' I said in return.

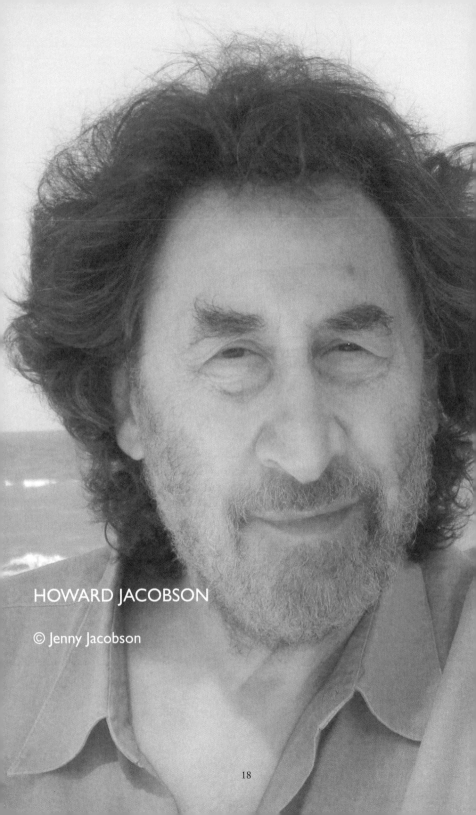

HOWARD JACOBSON

© Jenny Jacobson

In the old days when a publisher took one of his writers out to lunch he'd ask how the work was going. But now, like all publishers, Merton dreaded hearing. What if the work was going well? What if I had a book to show him? What if I was expecting an advance?

Eventually – as much to bring the afternoon to an end as to start a conversation, because the way things were going I would soon have no fingernails left, and because I cared for Merton and couldn't bear what he was going through – I said something. Not, *Christ, these chairs are uncomfortable, Merton*, not *Do you remember when you used to take me to L'Etoile and we ate cervelle de veau, not spotted dick?* but something more sympathetic to his state of mind. A couple of senior publishers – immediately castigated as dead white males – had gone public that weekend about the decline in the literacy of new writing: manuscripts turning up misspelt, ill-punctuated and ungrammatical, an uneducated jumble of mixed metaphors, dangling participles and misattributed apostrophes, less where there should have been fewer, mays where there should have been mights, mights where there should have been mays, theres for theirs and theirs for theres. We hadn't only forgotten how to sell books; we had forgotten how to write them. I didn't doubt that whatever else was at the root of Merton's depression, misattributed apostrophes weren't helping. 'You look,' I said, putting my paper napkin to my mouth, as though I too was in danger of losing teeth, 'like a man who hasn't read anything halfway decent for a long long time.'

I wanted him to see I understood it was hell for all of us.

'No, the opposite,' he said, probing the corners of his eyes with the tips of his fingers. He might have been trying to prise oysters out of their shells, except that he couldn't any longer afford oysters. 'The very opposite. The tragedy of it is, I've had at least twenty works of enduring genius land on my desk this month alone.'

Merton was famous for thinking that every novel submitted to him was a work of enduring genius. He was what was called a publisher of the old school. Finding works of enduring genius was why he'd entered publishing in the first place.

'Mmm,' I said.

Talking works of enduring genius made Merton almost garrulous. 'It would be no exaggeration,' he exaggerated, 'to say that eight or ten of them are masterpieces.'

I pulled a couple of hairs out of my moustache. '*That* good?'

'Breathtakingly good.'

Since none of these was mine, no matter what they said on Amazon, I had to labour to be excited for him. 'So where's the tragedy?' I asked, half hoping he'd tell me that the authors of at least four or five of them were dead.

But I knew the answer. None was suitable for three-for-two. None featured a vampire. None was about the Tudors. None could be marketed as a follow-up to *The Girl Who Ate Her Own Placenta*.

It was even possible that none was free of the charge of dangling a participle. Though Merton was a publisher of the old school, the new school – which held that a novel didn't have to be well written to be a masterpiece, indeed was more likely to be masterpiece for being ill-written – had begun to wear away his confidence. He didn't know what was what any more. And whatever was what, was not being submitted to him.

'Do you know what I am expected to require of you?' he suddenly looked me in the eyes and said. 'That you twit.'

'Twit?'

'Twit, tweet, I don't know.'

'And why are you expected to require it of me?'

'So that you can do our business for us. So that you can connect to your readers, tell them what you're writing, tell them where you're going to be speaking, tell them what you're reading, tell them what you're fucking eating.'

'Spotted dick.'

He didn't find that funny. 'So why particularly me?' I asked.

'Not just you. Everybody. Can you imagine asking Salinger to twit?'

'Salinger's dead.'

'No bloody wonder.'

He fell silent again, and then asked me if I used the Internet. *Used the Internet* – you had to love Merton, he was so out of touch.

'A bit.'

'Do you blag?'

'Blog? No.'

'Do you read other people's blags?'

'Blogs. Sometimes.'

'The blog's the end of everything,' he said.

The word sounded uncouth on his lips. It was like hearing the Archbishop of Canterbury talking about taking a Zumba class. The blog belongs to yesterday, I wanted to tell him. If you're going to blame anything you should be blaming myBlank and shitFace and whatever else was persuading the unRead to believe everybody had a right to an opinion. But it was rare to hear Merton open up and I didn't want to silence him almost before he'd begun. 'Tell me more,' I said.

He looked around the room as though he'd never seen it before. 'What's there to tell? Novels are history, not because no one can write them but because no one can read them. It's a different idea of language. Go on the Internet and all you'll find is –' He searched for a word.

I offered him expostulation. A favourite word of mine. It evoked the harumphings of bigoted old men. Only now it was the bigoted young who were harrumphing.

Merton seemed happy with it, in so far as he could be said to seem happy with anything. 'Novelists find their way to meaning,' he said. I nodded furiously. Wasn't I still finding my way to mine? But he was speaking to the unseen forces, not to me. 'The blog generation knows what it wants to say before it says it,' he continued.

'They think writing is opinionated statement. In the end that is all they will come to expect from words. My own children ask me what I mean all the time. They want to know what I'm getting at. They ask the point of the books I publish. What are they on about, Dad? Tell us so we don't have to read them. I can't come up with an answer. What's *Crime and Punishment* on about?'

'Crime and punishment.'

He didn't appreciate my facetiousness. 'So you think their question is fair? You think a novel is no more than its synopsis?'

'You know I don't.'

'Do you have children? I can't remember.'

'No.'

'You're lucky in that case. You don't have to see how badly educated they are. You don't have to see them come home from school having read a scene from *King Lear* – the one in the rain, it's not considered necessary to read about him when he's dry – and thinking they know the play. It's about this old fart, Dad.'

'So what do you say to them?'

'I say literature is not *about* things.'

'And what do they say?'

'That I'm an old fart.'

These were more words than I'd heard Merton utter in a decade. But they were to be his last. 'Mmm,' he said when he saw the bill. Later that afternoon, without twitting about it to anyone, he did what he had to do.

Howard Jacobson's *Zoo Time* was published September 2012 and is available in hardback, paperback, trade paperback and e-book editions. Reprinted with the kind permission of the author and Bloomsbury Publishing.

Author of the Man Booker Prize-winning *The Finkler Question*

Howard Jacobson
Zoo Time

ANDREW
McNEILLIE

POETRY

ANDREW McNEILLIE

In the wake of 'THE SEAFARER' [1]

I can sing you a song   about myself
tell of travels   toil and trouble
terrors on tossed waves   suffered at sea
(*you know I can*   *I've sung it before*)
night-watch nightmares   at the prow
crashing by cliffs   feet frozen
frost-bound   sea-weary
at hunger's door   soul-cares seething
hot round my heart.   The lucky lubber
has no idea   how I spent winter
(*from worst of November*)   in paths of exile
wretched and sorrowful   hung with icicles
hit by hail   on ice-cold sea
lost to the world.   Nothing but roar of icy waves

---

1. This version derives from the so-called 'Cill Mhuirbhigh Ms' attributed to the Árainn Scribe (fl.968-69) by Giraldus Cambrensis (?1146-?1220) who visited the island during his Irish travels. Giraldus claimed to have discovered it 'caulking a coracle', among other Mss whose thickness helped preserve it (BL Royal MS 13 B VIII (a)). Ida Gordon dismissed the entire text as 'irredeemably corrupt'. Little is known about the reputed scribe beyond a work on the age-old custom of *caoineadh* and that he stood fiercely opposed to institutionalised religion.

met my ears.   Only the swan's song
gannet, gull   and curlew cry
gave me pleasure   in adversity
not laughter   and drink at the bar.
Storms beat   wind-torn cliffs
icy-feathered   kittiwake called
dewy-feathered   the erne yelled.
No caring kin   can comfort the desolate heart.
Truly the burgher   merry with wine
flushed with pride   has no idea
what painful wandering   I must bide
and how often weary   endure
in the paths of the sea.   (*So I fare now*
aboard my glossary   battered by cruces
in ink-black night   chasing more than
imitation   more than word for word.
No comfy reader   turning pages
knows what pains I take   and pangs suffer
at heart for her. . .)
                    . . . Night-shadows darkened.
Snow fell from North   frost
gripped ground   hail hammered earth
coldest grain.   My heart-thoughts –
troubled   now I must venture
on high streams   of tumultuous brine –
urge me always   far from here
seeking homeland   of foreign folk.
No one on earth's   so proud of spirit
so generous of gifts   so bold in youth
brave-of-deed   dear to his love
he does not fear   what doom fate
might deal him at sea.   He has no time to think
of harp-throb   or receiving of rings
pleasure in woman   nor worldly things
or anything else   but waste of waters.
Who goes to sea   knows heart's care.
Groves blossom   burghs grow fair
meadows beautiful.   World quickens.

All things urge   spirit to embark
fare far   by flood-ways
though melancholy call   of summer's lord
the cuckoo bode   bitter heart-sorrow.
The lucky reader   blessed with comfort
does not know   suffering of those
who travel farthest   as far as they can go
in exile's ways.   So now my spirit flies
beyond my breast   over sea-flood
above whale-path   soars far and wide
to earth's four corners   – returning eager,
greedy for more   wildish destinies.[2]
The solitary flier's cry   urges irresistibly
the willing heart again   to take the whale-road.
And so for me   such heightened being
is hotter than   dead life on land.
I don't believe earth-wealth will   last forever.
Always without fail   one of three things
will render all uncertain   before the fatal hour:
disease or age   or sword-hate
rip life from those   doomed to die.
For every one praise   of the living is best
of children hereafter   for good deeds
against enmity   daring deeds
against evil ...

[*manuscript damaged* . . .][3]

Days all gone   of magnificence on earth.
There are no kings   no Caesars now
no gold-givers   without dirty money.
Now fallen all   that noble company.
Joys gone. Weaker men   wield world-power

---

2. 'géosceaft ge-wild'. Among her numerous caveats, Gordon protests 'a total want of authority' here.
3. Recent laboratory analysis indicates that sodium chloride residue from 'brine damage' here is of a density exclusive to that found along the western reaches of the N. Welsh coast, so opening up the proverbial can of worms.

thrive through trouble.   Glory fled.
Earth's nobility   grows old and sere
as shall every one   the world over.
Hoary-haired   old age comes on
faces grow pale.   We mourn old friends
sons of princes   given up to earth.
Body can't avail   when life leaves.
Can't swallow sweetness   nor feel pain
nor move hand   nor think with mind. . .

[*Here sea broke aboard   lines chopped through*
kennings cracked.   He spoke his last word
on the walkie-talkie   down with both hands in the ink
unwished for fate   for even your enemy . . .]

INTERVIEW

IMAGINING THE PATIENT

LITERATURE AND MEDICINE

Sue Charteris talks to Iona Heath

Iona Heath has just completed her term as President of the Royal College of GPs, and until recently worked as an inner city GP. Sue Charteris met Iona to find out about how her exploration of the relationship between literature and medicine informed her understanding of her patients' experience.

What started you reading and how do you fit it into your busy life?

I'd been in practice for fifteen years, so getting the hang of it a bit. At that point – it was 1989 – our practice decided that we would have a sabbatical programme of three months off every ten years, which was equivalent to giving each other an extra week's holiday. My children were primary school age so I couldn't really travel, and so instead I made this great plan to read novels in the morning and I was going to be a perfect mother in the afternoon – but that went by the board. [laughs]

How did you select what to read?

I was very scientific. I wrote to people I admired, and I asked them what ten books they would read if they could only read ten. And so I got absorbed in *Emma, Middlemarch, Bleak House, Anna Karenina…*

IONA HEATH

When you went back to work, how did you keep up with your new addiction?

I made a resolution that I would... I changed one of my half days so I could continue to read in the morning, which is my ideal luxury.

Chekhov, a doctor as well as a writer, talked about the ideal of a marriage between art and science...

He says it very beautifully and of course he is a consummate artist. The plays and the short stories are peerless. He writes about the sensitivity of the artist, that ability to sense – not only to listen – but to use *all* of the senses in assessing a situation, to take in the wholeness of it, and also about not censoring it to a scientific framework too early. At some point you need to go back to science but if you do it too soon, you'll make mistakes, make assumptions that are invalid. I've found the quotation:

I thought then that the sensitivity of the artist may equal the knowledge of the scientist. Both have the same object, nature and perhaps in time it will be possible for them to link together in a great and marvellous force which is at present hard to imagine.

Chekhov also says: 'The artist's responsibility is not to provide answers but to ask the right questions.' Art doesn't close down truth. Whereas science tends to...

In your consulting room, did your extensive reading make you more brave? I am thinking about the questions you asked your patients...

It's difficult to know, it wasn't a step change. I didn't go back and suddenly everything was completely different, but certainly I did become braver as time went by. How much of that is experience, and how much of that is reading? It's one of those things you learn. If you find a patient being tedious, it's usually your failure rather than theirs – you haven't asked the right questions, or you've not imagined it vividly enough. I used to teach students that you have to ask a leftfield question, a tangential question, to try and get them to come alive.

You have talked about the patient's search for meaning, the patient trying to relate to the language they think you, the doctor, will understand, and the two of you sense-making that language together.

It all comes down to language in the end, because the patient feels a sensation of something, and then they do the initial censoring, because they have to put that into language...

I remember in this context you quoting William Carlos Williams, another writer-doctor, from The Doctor Stories:

The physician enjoys a wonderful opportunity actually to witness the words being born. Their actual colours and shapes are laid before him carrying their tiny burdens which he is privileged to take into his care with their unspoiled newness.

And you talked about the way that patient's descriptions emerge out of the symptoms themselves. You are fascinated by the way that each individual chooses and uses words differently to describe those symptoms.

Yes, or they can't communicate it, and then the doctor has to show their understanding by finding words, not exactly the same words, not parroting, but we sometimes teach it as 'summarising': you're putting into words *your* understanding of what the patient is saying, to check back to see if that's right. Wordsworth describes a sort of joint sense-making in *The Prelude* that closely resembles this: 'and I would give, / While yet we may, as far as words can give, / Substance and life to what I feel'.

You tolerate a high level of ambiguity in your search for the patient's story.

That's certainly where I've learnt to put myself because nature is ambiguous. Human nature included. Our understanding, the totality of our understanding, is pathetic, compared with the reality. And so there's always a need to doubt what you know.

Some of the worst harms are done by making assumptions and thinking you know the answer when either you don't or there isn't an answer. You can't be completely fluid, but it should always be a provisional judgement and flexible. If you're too categorical, if you say 'This is going to happen and then this' and then it happens differently, the patient can lose trust or may leave treatment, and that can be disastrous.

Robert Frost described poetry as 'the shortest emotional distance between two points, the writer and the reader'. Can you say more for us what you would mean by 'emotional' distance? You're deliberately putting yourself apart from the scientific, objective, analytical training.

There's a very interesting phenomenon that you cannot be a doctor to your own children, because you cannot objectify them. You can tell whether other people's kids are seriously ill or not, but if it's your own kids, it's almost impossible. You've got so much emotion invested... You have to be able to oscillate – both the doctor and the patient must go backwards and forwards – between seeing the body and the mind as an object, which is when you are using science to look at what all objects have in *common*, and then as subject, where this is a completely *unique* body and mind. So you must keep trying to switch..

I'm interested in what you have to say about role boundaries, and, how you maintain your own wellbeing whilst staying empathetic and engaged.

Yes, easier said than done, and I think, sometimes we teach doctors to be too defensive, before they've got anywhere close to getting into dangerous areas. You can be emotionally exposed and open to what people are trying to tell you, but still be able to stand back and reason in a way that the person who's embroiled in illness can't. They may not have the knowledge to do it, but equally they may be overwhelmed. I think it's a sort of rational disengagement that's needed.

Does literature – having a wider cast of characters or drawing on different historical periods – help you stay more fresh to the possibilities of people, able to hear behind their words or the way they first appear?

I don't know if everybody does it but I walk around, you know, classifying people, 'that person reminds me of this person, who I've seen in this setting', you know, I look at people in the street and they remind me of certain patients...

[laughs] *Policemen are trained to do it!*

It's very useful – you have as a doctor to be able to recognise physiognomies and types of presentation, patterns of disease, limps and ways of moving the body that are slightly abnormal. You're sensitised to doing that. But of course it can lead to stereotyping. So it's how you do that discriminating *without* stereotyping. The more characters you have to draw on the more it helps. There's a wonderful bit in Timothy Mo's *Sour Sweet*, where he talks about this Chinese family, and the wife, when she speaks in English, she sounds strident and then there's a description of how she sounds in Chinese, and that, for example, was very helpful to me. We had a Chinese translator in the practice who seemed to me to be shouting at patients all the time, but I realised that maybe I needed to make an allowance that there's a different intonation in Chinese... I think cross-cultural reading is immensely helpful, reading novels from other cultures when you're dealing with a multicultural population. But then again it just gives you a wider set of stereotypes; it doesn't get rid of them altogether.

You are confronted with symptoms of poverty and deprivation quite often in your practice. It sounds like politics is coming into this but can you talk to us about the relationship between that and your choice of reading?

I think probably all great literature – there's a sweeping generalisation coming – all great literature deals, to some extent, with issues of justice. Dickens is an obvious example. So, two things can come from this. One is the dignity of the disadvantaged, the courage, the endurance, the capacity for survival that you can lose sight of when dealing with people who, in a way, are failing to cope. It's a very useful counterbalance consciously to look for that dignity. And the other thing you can find in literature is an analysis of the other side, an analysis of the posh boys... I think it helps you to make a bit more sense of what you're seeing.

You are unapologetic, as is John Berger, in what you call the avoidance of the rhetoric of otherness. He says

> **To try to understand the experience of another it is necessary to dismantle the world as seen from one's own place within it, and to reassemble it as seen from his. For example, to understand a given choice another makes, one must face in imagination the lack of choices which may confront or deny him**
> **(John Berger and Jean Mohr, *A Seventh Man* 1975)**

Can we talk more about John Berger and his influence on you because it seems to have been profound? I know that A Fortunate Man *is the most important book for you.*

Yes, my copy of *A Fortunate Man* is very precious because it's inscribed in the front. The first thing about my copy is that it says 'Iona McMillan, November 1969', which means I was nineteen-years-old, and I'd just started at medical school. I read it then and I thought it was wonderful. I read it again in 1989, twenty years later, and when I read it again I had no idea how I could have understood anything of what it was trying to say. I didn't understand what the nineteen-year-old me found in it really. But it resonated deeply. It's a wonderful book.

When I finally met John, he wrote in that first photograph: 'For Iona, this door which you know so well, and I a little, this door which opens onto what?' [See the picture on p.36]

Mohr's photograph is compelling, isn't it? The half-opened door of the surgery, and the light underneath, and that possibility that this is when the patient is telling him the most important thing. Do you think Berger knew how troubled Dr Sassall (real name John Eskell) 'the fortunate man' of the title was?

There's a wonderful film that was shown at the National Film Theatre recently, with John and Jean Mohr (the photographer) going through the photographs where they talk about it. It's not terribly clear but I think Sassall was known to have depression.

He struggled with boundaries didn't he? 'What if a patient presents me with something that I can't help with?'

Sassall was classically a perfectionist, wanting to do it well and do it right. He was such a thoughtful man and yes, from time to time he became deeply depressed. Depression amongst doctors is not a rarity.

You say in one of your lectures that cardiologists can at least be relieved their patient didn't die of heart disease but general practitioners don't have the luxury. Your patients are going to die, and you have to deal with the roundedness of that and the consequences of that.

Indeed. Berger wrote an afterword to the recent German edition:

> **When I wrote the preceding pages, and I'm thinking particularly of the last ones which speak of the impossibility of summing up Sassall's life and work, I did not know that fifteen years later he was going to shoot himself. Our instant Hedonist culture tends to believe that a suicide is a negative comment – what went wrong? it naively asks. Yet a suicide does not necessarily constitute a criticism of the life being ended, it may belong to that life's density. [typical John, that] This was the tragic Greek view. John the man I loved killed himself. And yes, his death has changed the story of his life; it has made it more mysterious, not darker. I see as much light there as ever. Simply more violently mysterious, this mystery makes me feel more modest as I stand before him, and standing before him I do not search for what I might have foreseen and didn't, as if the essential was missing from what passed between us. Rather, I now begin with his violent death and from it look back with increased tenderness on what he set out to do, and what he offered to others for as long as he could endure.**

Berger doesn't let the end of a life mar the beginning of it, which we so often do. Sassall had a complaint at the end, apparently, which was pretty much the last straw for him. Lots of doctors do commit suicide, and many of those cases are precipitated by complaints where somebody who has been striving their whole life to help is regarded as not having done what they should have done, or not having done it soon enough, or not being prescient enough. Some take complaints very much to heart.

If you're not rationalising what is possible, emotionally and mentally, and instead thinking you might be able to solve everything the patient presents you with, you are setting yourself very high standards.

I've been talking about it recently, David Rieff's book on the death of Susan Sontag. It's a son's memoir – Susan Sontag is his mother. She was determined she was going to beat her disease and he fears that he colluded with her in this hope or fantasy. She took all these dreadful treatments, and David asks why no doctor was courageous enough to say 'no' to her.

It's interesting that we come to Susan Sontag because she too pays great tribute to John Berger:

He writes about what is important, not just about what is interesting. In contemporary English letters he seems to me peerless; not since Lawrence has there been a writer who offers such attentiveness to the sensual world with responsiveness to the imperatives of conscience.

Last question. What three books you would take on your desert island?

The Oxford English Dictionary because words are so fascinating; Berger's *A Fortunate Man* because it's so entrenched in my work and my everything, and because it's set me off on a lot of other paths, and I love everything he writes. A third book. It's impossible to choose. It would probably be *War and Peace*. Yes, it needs to be something you could read again and again and find different things in each time. It would probably be *War and Peace*. I'll change my mind again in a minute...

POETRY

CHRIS HARDY

Making Ready

On the wall of the room
opposite the door

is a mirror,
so when entering I meet

someone trying to leave
who has not been me for years.

After clearing the furniture
to get at the floor

I see the walls need mending too
and wonder if it's worth it.

I like the emptied room,
its squares of pale colour

where pictures hung,
like windows in the darkened paint,

as if the light that filled this space
when we first walked in had

crept behind the frames and slept.
I'd throw out everything if I could,

leave the room with nothing in it,
only a door and in another wall

a window, through which I see
the sky shine and move, also a tree.

ESSAY

NOTE ON PULSATION AND POETRY

Seán Haldane

Pulsation is defined in the Oxford English Dictionary as: 'Rhythmical expansion and contraction; beating, throbbing, vibration.' Oscillate is defined as: 'Swing to and fro. Vibrate.' But the German Wahrig Dictionary provides a clear distinction between Pulsation and Oscillation. Pulsation is (I translate): 'Activity of the heart; the consequently evident pressure-waves in the arterial vascular system'. Oscillation is: 'Swinging: regular movements'.

Oscillation, for example in a twanging guitar string or a pendulum, is regular and 'equal phase'. Pulsation is, like the heartbeat, 'unequal phase'. It can be used to distinguish the living (e.g. a jellyfish) from the non-living (e.g. a ringing bell). Graphs of electrocardiograms (ECG) and brain blood oxygenation show an unequal-phase rise and fall. If you pay attention to your (or any animal's) breathing you will see that in-breath and out-breath (unless under extreme stress in panting or gasping) are unequal phase with a ratio of about 2:3.

Pulsation is a sign of life in music and in poetry too – except often for 'free verse' which risks not being poetry at all unless its rhythms are strong enough to carry emotion as pulsation does.

Robert Graves wrote about 'Anvil and Oar' in stressed verse. The guiding tap or taps from the blacksmith's small hammer preceding the bang from the apprentice's sledgehammer form something like a Greek Iambic, and in ancient Ireland Brigit was the goddess of poets and blacksmiths. The pull of the oars in Anglo-Saxon and Viking boats matches the *Beowulf* four-stress line.

Superficially the *Beowulf* line is 'equal phase' – two stresses / two stresses. But although Olympic rowers may use a technique allowing two breaths per stroke, in normal rowing you breathe *in* on the 'recovery' (when you push the oars forward with the blades out of the water), then *out* on the longer phased 'drive' when you pull the oar towards you through the water.

In the following two lines from *The Battle of Maldon*, each stress with its following syllable or syllables is itself an unequal-phase pulsation. At first this seems in reverse because we think of in-breath then out-breath, but if you think of the stressed (marked) syllable as corresponding with the out-breath on the drive, and the unstressed syllable(s) as the in-breath on the recovery, each stress is longer than the unstressed phase. (And note how each stress is linked to others by alliteration). You can imagine fast rowing:

Tha **Byhrt**noth **brace**-d **bill** of **scethe**,
Brad and **brun**eccg, and on the **byrn**an **sloh**.

[Then Byrthnoth drew his sword from his sheath
Broad and bright-bladed, and on the chainmail struck.]

The Old Irish poetry cited by Graves typically has lines of seven syllables. In the Late Middle Ages Irish poetry adopted new stress metres from French and English sources but the syllabic metres still survive, e.g. in many of the modern Scottish Gaelic poems of Sorley MacLean. These metres contain various rhyming and alliteration patterns which link the last syllables and middle syllables of alternating lines – the middle syllable of a seven-syllable line being either the third or the fourth. This creates a sort of pulsation and counter-pulsation, expressive of changing emotion.

The 5-stress line which has settled itself into English (not exactly an 'iambic pentameter', as is sometimes taught, because it may contain extra syllables and reversals which break the metrical 'tum-ti-tum-ti-tum-ti' effect) typically has an unequal phase rise and fall. It is remarkably like a breath (human or animal) in that there is a slight fall in tone after the second stress. Take Shakespeare's

> When **I** do <u>**count**</u> the **clock** that **tells** the **time**
> And **see** the <u>**brave**</u> **day** sunk in **hid**eous **night**.

Shakespeare varies the 'tum-ti-tum' of the five stresses, but both lines follow the 2:3 ratio of the breathing pulsation, with a slight lilt I have marked by the underlined words.

Furthermore each stress in a 5-stress line roughly equates to a heartbeat, i.e. 5 beats to a line.

Since average respiration rate is 12 to 15 breaths a minute, and average heartbeat is about 68, a sonnet at 14-lines long and 70 stress-beats takes almost exactly a minute to read! A sonnet is 14 breaths and 70 heartbeats. A sonnet is a minute. Why this coincidence?

I can't answer the question, but I can point to the phenomenon. Perhaps a study of poetic forms would reveal other such correspondences between them and biological pulsation.

THE READING REVOLUTION

A MANIFESTO FOR CRILS AT CHRISTMAS

Philip Davis

The unit for research into reading that we set up in Liverpool is just over a year old now. It is called CRILS – the Centre for Research into Reading, Information and Linguistic Systems. Odd though perhaps it may seem at first, we came out of a department for the study of English literature and into a faculty of Health and Life Sciences, to widen our remit across disciplines and in relation to the world outside.

What do we do there?

Part of what we do, in collaboration with psychologists, health professionals, sociologists and statisticians, is seek to evaluate the outreach work of The Reader Organisation, the shared reading-aloud of literature that goes on in groups created everywhere and anywhere – within libraries, prisons, drug-rehabilitation centres, dementia care-homes, schools, and so on. If what we call The Reading Revolution is to take its place in the national agenda and win both support and funding, then it is vital that its claims are rigorously tested by both qualitative and quantitative analysis. That means questionnaires, interviews, transcripts, recordings and filmings, brain-imaging, control trials, measures of well-being, graphs, calculations of costs and savings – a mixed methodology.

But it is equally important that the individuals within the unit keep coming back to their own reading and writing.

Otherwise we become merely second-order specialists, thinking all too generally *about* reading rather than thinking within it. Reading is not simply an activity for its own sake any more than books are self-enclosed objects: the process and the text alike give way to the content, the meaning and the purpose, the life of thought and feeling they serve to create and imagine. So, for example, I am working on a new series for Oxford University Press called *The Literary Agenda*, on what reading literature should mean in the twenty-first century, with very specific examples; Josie Billington is continuing her work on the poet Elizabeth Barrett Browning with an edition to follow up on her recent book *Elizabeth Barrett Browning and Shakespeare*; Paul Watry is working on the digital technology of the future and on the understanding of complex data.

Still, we have recently been asking ourselves to ponder a large statement made by an early twentieth-century researcher, Edmund Huey, who travelled the United States investigating the teaching and practice of reading:

And so to completely analyse what we do when we read would almost be the acme of a psychologist's achievements, for it would be to describe very many of the most intricate workings of the human mind, as well as to unravel the tangled story of the most remarkable specific performance that civilization has learned in all its history.

We aim to increase the status and understanding of literary reading as an emotionally exploratory area for thinking, in ways that are often both unrecognised within the formal study of literature and under-rated in the wider world. The question we have been asking ourselves is how to do 'research' into reading that would be exciting, imaginative, and meaningful, not merely generalised, or dry, or pious. Here are some preliminary notes and attempts at an answer.

Background

'Research' in the humanities characteristically has to do with editing the work of an author, or writing a biography or study, but mainly arises out of ideas emergent from within the human texture and situation created inside the books. That these ideas might be susceptible to experiment, testing and proof is not the conceptual or disciplinary norm as it might be in science.

What adds to the difficulty is something like a serious historical embarrassment. That is to say, academic literary study is too often now a rather self-enclosed place of specialisation – the more ironic since its subject-matter, literature itself, is the very opposite in its reach and purpose. CRILS exists in counter-response to that process of division of labour and the specialisation of separated disciplines which has gained ever-increasing momentum from the nineteenth century onwards. Its main argument is that literature serves as a central human reservoir or holding-ground for meaning and for uncertainty, in resistance to those tendencies towards separation, alienation and dispersal. It is important that literary people and literary reading-groups exist such that their very existence represents a challenge to demarcation. Nonetheless it is awkward that the content of the study of literature – which previously might have been a part of religion, then a part of morality, then a part of education – is now given its best chance as part of health and well-being. But literature is not simply 'healthy' or even 'therapeutic', though it does enable thoughts to be thought that would not otherwise find a place for themselves as proper subject-matter within a specific discipline.

Perhaps this historical shift does not matter too much; human content must exist within whatever forms it can and seek transcendence from within them. That potential transcendence is one of the objects of study: content over form (albeit realised through form), individual over limited or damaged situation, reality over institutional framework, primary detail over secondary categories.

The real question may be how far, as an exploratory and meditative holding-ground for human meaning, the reading of literature can become some kind of modern collaborative successor to the purposes of dogmatic religion, or formal philosophy and practical psychology.

What to do, in order to think harder about these matters?

Question 1: What really happens when we read?

Wordsworth spoke of remembering *how* he felt at a particular time, but *what* exactly he felt he did not recall. Attention in reading may be directed towards the 'what' of the text, but the exploratory and meditative process that goes on in the background is arguably just as important though probably less conscious. The 'how' of reading may be not just an instrumental means to an end but an intrinsic part of an experience, a way of thinking and a place for thinking that the world does not usually create or encourage.

What mental processes are involved that make immersed reading in serious literature different from ordinary thinking? (Including here the relation of emotion to thought in the moment, as part of recovered human wholeness).

Is there such a thing (a function of being) which may be called 'a reader' – a searcher for meaning, say?

Trials can do something towards comparing reading a newspaper, a self-help book, and a literary work. There is some empirical evidence to show that slowing of reading is involved here and David Miall (and others in what is known as empirical aesthetics) have shown that distinctive literary features regularly produce that slowing effect even amongst readers without a strong literary background.

a) *Transcripts* from the reading-groups rely as much on the literary analysis of human discourse as do the texts the reading groups are actually looking at, in order to discover the transient quality and unexamined nature of the encounter. These transcripts take us very close to the momentary reality of what is actually happening but with the added dimension of time for reflection. It is possible to identify breakthroughs as well as resistances and missed opportunities; the intuitive development of mental tools; indicators of change or suddenness of realisation. As far as I am aware, no one else is doing this work in this particular area.

b) *Brain-imaging experimentation* into the relation of syntax in front of one's eyes to the shift and configuration of mental pathways behind them. The shape and motion of an utterance of emotional importance may have a powerful effect in preventing the hardening of mental arteries, the re-enforcement of set opinions and agendas in isolation from immersion in the praxis of contingent human existence. It is argued that literature is the best model we have for the raw unpredictability of such existence – not that literature is itself uncontrolled, unmediated and raw but that within its structures is created the dynamic for the generation of rich complexity beyond obvious preconceptions.

c) *The experience of sudden 'called-for' thoughts.* The Victorian fantasy writer George MacDonald praised Wordsworth not so much for his ideas as for locating the place (in nature, in mind, in a specific human situation) in which the thoughts arose. The creation of such a place, like a saturated solution of meaning in a crucible so to speak, is what literature does as its own version of experimentation. That means that thoughts are not like the dry residue of experience, are not static knowledge ready to be employed to categorise a situation: in literature such preconceptions have to be kept to the back of one's mind, forgotten unless triggered and activated again with appropriate modifications arising out of the immediate specifics. Thoughts must arise out of felt need, out of sudden excited recognition or new configuration, in some relation between a very specifically testing situation and the tacit store of mind in immersed response. This is like the sort of counselling session envisaged by the psychoanalyst Bion in *Attention and Interpretation*, where nothing should be taken-for-granted – only here the reader is more freely his or her own therapist prompted to take different and varied relations in relation to himself or herself (or other implicatingly imagined selves), and finding inner voices operating tacitly between self and book, through the interactive triggers of the text.

d) *The power of the language.* In comparison with a non-literary language which is simply instrumental/informative/opinionated, what does the power of a literary language do, in terms of resonance, of surrounding but not explicitly spoken thoughts which nonetheless get into the reader's head when the reader is imaginative?

Initial action-point: We apply for a grant to compare reading a literary work with reading a self-help manual (on, say, depression) or a newspaper, all within group-settings.

The hypothesis is that:

a) Literary reading is implicit psychotherapy, all the more effective in relation to existential problems (which are too often ignored by psychologists because incurable as such) for *not* providing a cure in terms of 'self-help'.

b) Current-affairs discussions arising out of newspaper-reading would be arguably less deep, more opinionated in advance and contentious rather than socially and humanly binding and deepening.

c) Literary reading serves as a means of actualising key human concerns emotionally in ways that, for once, let them *out*: offering through the admission of literature a means of handling them (by way of resolving, not solving); a way of gaining experience in what was not initially or always recognised as worthy of the name 'experience', perhaps because too small or humiliating, or too much to do with loss or absence; a means of preventing oneself becoming desensitised to such matters.

Question 2: How is it possible to do research into both the existential models and the existential environments that reading literature creates, as alternative worlds?

Some remarks above should have provided indicators that characterise the literary experience (though of course we are aware that this is our version of such an experience and there are others): e.g. not knowing in advance; slowed deep thinking in intrinsic relation to personal emotion and intuition; melting-pots or saturated solutions full of more than allows for stereotyped response; the text not as a two-dimensional manual but more like a living presence or person that means something not easily summarised or dismissed; the transcendence of meaning.

In the course of our work we in CRILS find ourselves interested in one thing existing inside its apparent opposite. That is to say, we are interested in settings, mental and social, which being safe defend *un*safe thoughts and allow them to be held. Or again, where lost primary realities in their rawness and naivety – for example, the need to find speech, to cry out or confess, or the need for counsel, support or kinship – can find properly secondary forms such as literature in which to have presence again even amidst further complications and subtleties. Most

"Literature says... Nothing human is alien from me"

of our reality is habitual, blindly normalising, under-emotional, and not as safe as we suppose in terms of the needs and pains it represses as the price of keeping going. The creation of a mental place, and within it an imaginatively simulated human model, for a fuller registering of existence and a richer form of human being is the aim here in the broadest sense of health. We cannot get there on our own: we need the booster-rocket of literature to *remind us* of feelings, capabilities, situations, privately repressed realities not generally acknowledged in the current social order. Literature says there are no 'cases': nothing human is alien from me.

The assumption here is that art is not that special in kind, albeit special in degree. 'Poetry' begins in real life-forms when, say, a patient stutters and stumbles amidst words, verbal options, in order to make best sense of his or her problem. Or it begins when a vulnerable thing, which might seem to have no acceptable place in the world, finds a sufficiently strong resistant or compelling language to have it admitted into acknowledged reality rather than dismissed. That is art's hard-earned gift of protection, defence and representation on behalf of the race.

Initial action-point: one aim might be to look at moments of break-through in reading-groups and by recording (oral/visual), ask participants to reflect upon the session and see if those moments are picked out again by them. This bridges the gap between the micro-level of something suddenly happening in a deep emotional environment and the macro-level of understanding thereafter in the norms of the world.

Question 3: Do we need something more than (or after) private reading?

There is clearly research somehow to be done on the relation of the shared reading (read aloud) model and the internalised voicings of private reading – their differences, the question also as to whether the former can lead group-members back to the latter, and whether it remains necessary even so to continue the community of group-reading.

There are further intricate questions about inner and external reading voices, especially when they're happening simultaneously.

But this is also arguably part of a wider question: how is private reading to have a role in the public, social world? It is easy to see art as an optional extra, as though for leisurely pastime or private consumption by processes of division and alienation. This view is a symptom of that loss of wholeness which literature itself characteristically seeks to overcome. What is more, the transfer of the literary into the real seems to be something a realist literary fiction such as *Middlemarch* implicitly demands of its readers, even when the practical means and process of translation may not be clear.

Literature seeks a place in the world – and a role in changing human being in the world. This may be a practical argument for readers-in-residence as human agents in a number of different settings in a different ordering of humane social provision including education in the modern world, but it is also more than that – namely, the challenge to make literature actively real in its effects upon people.

How can this be a matter for a research or development programme, for experiment or testing? Perhaps we need to help create a model – a building and an environment – for a social centre that transforms libraries, educational facilities, and psychological provision, in practical and physical refutation of scepticism about such idealistic possibilities.

POETRY

EMMA CURRAN

Mermaid's Purses

Discarded evidence
of the life of the sea,
kept like caul. This shore
is sentimental, has stored
her memento on a shelf
of rock, on the mantelpiece
of the beach. I know
this impulse well enough,
recognise that this crisp
thin shell reminds of a time
beneath water, tells how once
it swelled with beginnings.

On the River

Brought to me on the river,
flotsam of half-remembered
words and phrases floating
over the waved and blurred
surface, hypnotising until
I fall under, reliving where
I'd imagined I'd submerged.
I meet again those bridges
I thought I'd already crossed
or wouldn't ever have to. Signs
for 'no fishing' mean nothing
in this deep dredging. The silt
of old beds unsettled, a tangle
of weeds to cling and drown,
here where sounds are not
as they began and shadows can't
seem to fall straight in new light.

Canal Life

Narrowboats are slow along the canal.
Floral painted panels name them all –

three 'Elizabeth's in a row
shimmy into the lock.

The keeper can fit these few,
his livestock in a pen of sorts.

The bridge clicks closed together;
its halves wholed in a handhold.

The windows eye each other,
prows in Pisces, three
mirroring living rooms.

The levelling of water, measured
liquid breath – inhalation, exhalation –
lends each Elizabeth the equilibrium

she needs to keep going.
The lines and gauges show
enough given, enough taken

for boats to part company then,
a scattering shoal darting
the river with individual colours.

THE READING REVOLUTION

A CAPTIVE AUDIENCE

Alexis McNay

So attentive and engaged are the audience, so astute the questions, this might have been a reading on the circuit but for the elaborate handshakes being exchanged at the end between the circle of men and, at their centre, the poet, Brian Turner.

Turner, an American ex-serviceman who served as an infantry team leader in Iraq between 2003 and 2004, and whose experiences there provided the raw material for two very powerful and important collections of poetry, has come to do two readings at Walton prison for an event organized by The Reader Organisation in partnership with Writing on the Wall, HMP Liverpool and Manchester College. It is such a success that the Arts Council have happily funded The Reader Organisation to coordinate a national pilot between five literature festivals and prisons or secure mental health-care facilities in their area.

'Soldier-poet' is a title with which Brian Turner is not entirely comfortable, though he accepts that, little as it can describe him in depth, it does provide a tag by way of which his work can be broadly understood. But that tension – on one hand the soldier defined by physicality and aggression, on the other, the soul refined by emotion and sensitivity – seems particularly

BRIAN TURNER

PHANTOM NOISE

resonant in prison. It is a tension explored and reconciled in the weekly 'R&R' (Read and Relax) groups delivered by The Reader Organisation, and it perhaps accounts for the immediate rapport and recognition between Turner and his audience. As he walks through the wings, he says 'these men look just like my squaddies'; as he launches into 'The Hurt Locker', his first poem of the day,

Nothing but hurt left here.
Nothing but bullets and pain
and the bled-out slumping
and all the *fucks* and *goddams*
and *Jesus Christs* of the wounded.
Nothing left here but the hurt.

the men in the room are transfixed. The photocopy of the poem they've been given hangs limp in their hands; they are watching the poet as he recites.

Brian Turner's morning session is on the Vulnerable Prisoner wing, which is usually overlooked by events of this kind – this poetry reading is a first. The audience, made up of the weekly R&R group members, are appreciative, respectful, and do every justice to this privilege. But they are also keen to get as much as they can out of the occasion – the best kind of audience – and the convivial recital-discussion format allows a direct dialogue between the poet, the poetry and the men. Two hours pass quickly, and the range of discussions, reactions, and positive contacts inspired says much for what this kind of event can offer in prison. No, it says how much these men can offer this kind of event. Men who are aspiring poets are inspired by seeing a poet at work and join in discussion about how rhythm works. There are thoughtful reflections on what is analogous between the poet's experiences and the men's own. There are informed questions relating to geostrategy and politics. And there are en-dorsements of the importance of literature to life on the most fundamental and profound level. Turner reads '2000 lbs', a poem which describes the impact of a roadside bomb in terms of the diverse lives, all with their own thoughts, pasts and potential futures, which it obliterates. One of the verses tells of a 'Lt Jackson', who 'stares at his missing hands… these absurd stumps held in the air / where just a moment before he'd blown bubbles / out the Humvee window… something for the children, something beautiful'. Turner finishes the poem and a little way into discussion a man wants to know whether Lt Jackson came out alright. His concern extends to the poet as he adds 'if you don't mind me asking?' Turner doesn't duck any questions, but he hesitates a moment on this, before replying, 'let's just say he wasn't OK'.

The afternoon reading takes place in the chapel, perched, airy and serene, on top of G wing. It's slightly more formal, beginning with an hour-long reading, and some staff are apprehensive about attention levels. There is no problem. Turner's ease and authenticity, the power of the poems, the engagement and generosity of the audience, the will, again, to *make the most of*, are forces more powerful than mere bladders or nicotine cravings. The tenor of the questions matches the morning's, too, on the whole. There is one man who asks what perhaps a few are wondering; 'how many did you kill?'. A moment's reflection, and Turner answers, '1.2 million', before expanding with the suggestion that from the person pulling the trigger to the people paying the taxes, we're all implicated in *all* the deaths. It's a fitting end to what has been a thought-provoking day. We look forward to the next.

This article was originally published in the prison newspaper *Inside Time*

THE READING REVOLUTION

POETIC JUSTICE

A NARRATIVE OF BELFAST BREAKTHROUGHS

Patricia Canning

That's shit'. So says J, a middle-aged woman, of Shakespeare's sonnet 29 at my Get Into Reading group at a Belfast prison. 'What bits are particularly shit?' I ask. 'Well, all of it. Who talks like that, anyway?' Turns out, after a bit of unpacking and a long discussion on the fine line between free will and necessity, it's not 'shit', just *difficult*. 'You always think the grass is greener on the other side, don't you – but it isn't', says L, a woman whom I know to be speaking from experience. Applying the text to real life, another of the group says of the opening line 'When in disgrace with fortune and men's eyes', 'I'm expecting to be treated like that, when I leave here'. Such musings could be the modern day equivalent of Shakespeare's Richard III, 'And every tale condemns me for a villain'. Certainly, that's how our friend has been feeling. Another woman whose brash, public face belies a sensitive acknowledgement of her 'outcast state' offers this: 'I spend hours, sometimes, crying in my cell – just like [the speaker]'. Finally, like a light going on in the mind of our friend (she of the excremental analogy), J delightedly exclaims, 'Oh! I get it – it's about jealousy and depression!'

Every week I read with these women – women for whom life has been difficult, unbearable, even, and for whom society has assigned a role that they, like characters straight out of a

Shakespearean tragedy, feel obliged to play. 'For how long, though?' is the question that comes from reading the sonnet together. J's assertion that 'I will always be the woman who has been in prison', is met with aggressive sincerity by K: 'Change how you think about it, like the man in the poem... you need to find that *thing* to keep you going'. It's bloody hard here, but K is right – there are things that keep you going.

It seems such a simple thing, really. Every week, I – or sometimes, the women – read short stories and poems, aloud, together. We talk about the texts in ways that relate fictional life stories to our real ones in numerous and often offbeat ways. I say 'real', but they're not always our real stories. Sometimes, they are the lives and stories we wish we had – or didn't have. I'm often asked what it is that Get Into Reading *does* for the women. My initial thought is usually an acknowledgement of the appropriateness of the verb, 'doing' – it is true, however unintentional the material implication may be, that Get Into Reading 'does' something. It has very practical applications. Let me try and put into words what that very real, practical *thing* is.

In the first session, P, an imposing woman who is a self-confessed non-reader with limited social skills, became agitated as soon as the staff officer left. P was either unable or unwilling to express what the matter was – perhaps the closing of the door, however well-meaning, was understood as another form of imprisonment. I wondered, then how she would feel about my reading choice that day, a delightful short story ('Faith and Hope Go Shopping' by Joanne Harris) about two elderly ladies conspiring together to escape the constraints of their care home to travel to London in search of their holy grail – a pair of 'inappropriate' shiny, red designer shoes. P, as if sensing my interest, demanded to leave both the room and the project. I tried, without success, to encourage her to stay for a bit before making that decision. She reluctantly agreed to sit the session out, only because there was no-one to escort her back to her cell. To underscore the point, she turned her back on me, and the rest of the group. In the absence of a more practical solution, I simply started reading. Before long, it was clear that there were parallels between the well-meaning staff at the fictional care-home and the prison, in that our heroines had been 'banned' from reading material that would presumably (or presumptuously) incite rebellion, in action or in thought. In the story, *Lolita* was on the banned list. For their own good, you understand. In a clear case of life mirroring art, I too had been cautioned by some of the staff to avoid stories about 'sensitive subjects', such as prison or murder and 'anything that will upset them' (all without qualification). I wondered if 'Faith and Hope' was to be our *Lolita*. I read for a bit and after stopping at a few points and sharing some discussion with the rest of the group, I cast a surreptitious glance at P, and noted that she had slowly, almost in spite of herself, started to turn around. It was clear that she was trying to participate. Five minutes later, at a point of quiet reflection on the text, she leaned into the group, and in a barely audible voice, whispered, 'I really like this'. The spontaneous applause that followed from her fellow group members, expressed as much of my own relief and gratitude as it did theirs.

Six weeks in, P was still there. I remember that week vividly. I read 'The Story of an Hour', by Kate Chopin, which tells of a woman whose husband is understood to have died in an accident. As the news is reported to the woman she struggles with conflicting feelings of grief and relief, which in the story, are presented collectively as one entity, a tangible 'thing' that advances towards her, and which threatens to overwhelm her. P, who is serving a sentence for the manslaughter of a violent partner, was getting very restless. Something, not yet understood, was happening to her as I read the following passage:

There was something coming to her and she was waiting for it, fearfully. What was it? She did not know; it was too subtle and elusive to name. But she felt it, creeping out of the sky, reaching toward her through the sounds, the scents, the color that filled the air.

Now her bosom rose and fell tumultuously. She was beginning to recognise this thing that was approaching to possess her, and she was striving to beat it back with her will – as powerless as her two white slender hands would have been. When she abandoned herself

a little whispered word escaped her slightly parted lips. She said it over and over under her breath: 'free, free, free!' The vacant stare and the look of terror that had followed it went from her eyes. They stayed keen and bright. Her pulses beat fast, and the coursing blood warmed and relaxed every inch of her body.

Throughout the reading, I was conscious of P's increasing agitation, and of something visibly present that I would later recall as pain – I could see it. It was etched on her face as she tried desperately to communicate *something*. I stopped to give her the opportunity to speak and what followed was a series of incoherent and disjointed sentences that, when put together said, simply, 'That's how I feel'. I have never watched another person who has all of the physiological workings and cognitive apparatus necessary to enable speech, struggle so much to articulate a statement before that moment. But what a statement. With some gentle encouragement, she attempted, many times, to recount through a broken narrative, the circumstances that led her to prison and the emotional struggle she has experienced every day since. Words like 'pain', 'guilty', 'love', 'loss', surfaced alongside bits of sentences; 'miss him', 'feel guilt', 'can't grieve'. The only sentence that came with any clarity was 'that's how I feel'. To be able to express an emotion or a thought is half the battle when it comes to dealing with the ramifications of that emotion or thought. As Fernando Pessoa puts it, in his wonderful *The Book Of Disquiet*, 'To express something is to conserve its virtue and take away its terror'.

P's story is not unusual. Neither is the utility of the text in this way. Yesterday, for example, I read with a group, ex-prisoners, men, who have spent a lifetime in jail. One of the men, S, said afterwards, 'You know, Patricia, I can see why you read like this in prison. We are not *reading* the text here – we're *investigating* it'. To use his words, 'we're looking at all the angles'. We read Morley Callaghan's 'The Snob', a story about a young student overcome by shame and humiliation at encountering – and ignoring - his scruffy father in a bookshop, to prevent his girl from suffering the indignity of having to meet him. Yet it is he who passes judgement on his own family. 'That girl wasn't given a chance to form her own opinion', said our man. 'He formed it for her'. Having spent time discussing why that might be, the guys concluded that society, epitomised in our protagonist, has a lot to answer for.

Another week, and H, who has spent 26 years in prison, 15 of them 'in solitary', read Charlotte Mew's poem, 'The Call', to the group after we had read it once over and talked about what or who had made 'the call':

> **Was it a bright or a dark angel? Who can know?**
> **It left no mark upon the snow,**
> **But suddenly it snapped the chain**
> **Unbarred, flung wide the door**
> **Which will not shut again;**
> **And so we cannot sit here any more.**
> **We must arise and go:**
> **The world is cold without**
> **And dark and hedged about**
> **With mystery and enmity and doubt,**
> **But we must go**
> **Though yet we do not know**
> **Who called, or what marks we shall leave upon the snow.**

'That could be anything', said H. 'It could be the end of something or someone and you have no choice but to get on with it without them'. 'Aye', responds S, 'But it could be a good thing – a new start – cutting the dead wood and moving on'. H asked if he could keep the poem. 'I want to read it again later', he says. At the end of that particular session we were interrupted by a big wall of a man who came in to the group because he was fed up waiting outside on S (we had overrun). Taking a copy of the poem as I was about to read it, he reads along with me. 'Wow, that could mean a thousand things!' he says of Mew's poem. He goes on to give a very articulate and profound interpretation of 'The Call' before apologising when he suddenly becomes aware of the sound of his own voice. 'Sorry love, for sticking my nose in'. We encourage him to continue and afterwards, the guys and I invite him to next week's session. His response was reminiscent of a Monty Python sketch; 'Jesus, no' he exclaims, 'I don't read poetry or books!'

Our guys don't read books so much as they read people. 'If you don't, you get stroked', says H, 'pretty soon you're a dead man'. This kind of 'reading of humans' has helped H to extrapolate from the intricacies of the literary readings. He will seize on words that others often overlook and attribute to them a contextual significance that shapes and enriches our readings of the characters. While discussing a short story about a confrontation between a thuggish dad and a middle class university professor in a park, H hesitates over the word 'incredible' in the sentence describing the latter's wife's reaction:

Would there be violence, fighting? How dreadful, how incredible…She must do something, stop them call for help

H claims the word 'incredible' 'doesn't fit with the wife's disgust at the violence'. Actually, it doesn't – its juxtaposition with 'dreadful' is incongruent. 'She's scared that they'll fight, but at the same time she's excited by it', asserts H; 'she wants him to get stuck in 'cos she's fed up with her boring life with him'. Nods of agreement from the rest of the group follow as does a scramble for 'evidence' of H's synopsis from the text itself. At the end of the story H tells us that 'this story has actually changed my thinking… I would never normally walk away from a challenge, but you can see, here, how fighting this guy will achieve nothing – in fact, walking away is harder, but it actually is the right thing, even if it doesn't please everyone'. Seeing 'all the angles' is key to H's revelation and change of attitude. He tells me so at the end. The totality of the story offers just that – beginning, middle, end. A chance to think things through. The reading allows us time for reflection on an event before it happens in reality, or, conversely, to reconsider a similar past event and make a more objective assessment of our handling of it.

Back at the prison, and P has gone on from barely speaking to mentoring others in basic literacy. Recently she took me aside and asked, 'Patricia, whatever happened at the end of that story you read with us, you know, the one with the woman who has to go underground because of a bomb or something?' She was referring to H. C. Neal's 'Who Shall Dwell', which I read with her almost 2 years ago, when she was barely able to deal with even basic social contact. I told her the name of the story and she squealed 'that's it! I missed the end of that for some reason and I often think about it – I've always wanted to know what happened to that family.' The family to which she refers lives under threat of a nuclear attack and build a bomb shelter as a safe haven for their small family. When safely inside with four minutes to impact, the mother succumbs to the desperate calls from outside, momentarily opens the door and surrenders her place to a child who would have otherwise died. Unable or unwilling to take steps to reverse the situation, the father, too, opens the door, throws another two children inside the shelter instructing his son not to open the door 'for at least a week', before inevitably perishing with his wife. Looking back over my records I noted that P had attended the full session, but for whatever reason, had no recollection of the story's conclusion. For her, the story raised concerns about the people 'left behind' and the impossible situation in which the mother finds herself. Our discussions raised questions about whether this couple are playing God (the title invokes Psalm 15, 'who shall dwell in thy holy hill'), or merely taking charge of their own destiny. These questions have a particular significance for our group. P, for her part, has had to learn to take control of things, to make decisions that will, in the first instance, help herself. It hasn't been easy. As she left, she hugged me and whispered very quietly, 'thank you – it's been tough, but I've come a long way, Patricia'.

Bloody right, she has.

POETRY

THE OLD POEM

Brian Nellist

William Shakespeare (1564-1616)
***Love's Labours Lost*, 'Song'**

When icicles hang by the wall,
   And Dick the shepherd blows his nail,
And Tom bears logs into the hall,
   And milk comes frozen home in pail,
When blood is nipped, and ways be foul,
Then nightly sings the staring owl,
      To-whit;
     To-who, a merry note,
While greasy Joan doth keel the pot.

When all around the wind doth blow,
   And coughing drowns the parson's saw,
And birds sit brooding in the snow,
   And Marian's nose looks red and raw,
When toasted crabs hiss in the bowl,
Then nightly sings the staring owl,
      To-whit;
     To-who, a merry note,
While greasy Joan doth keel the pot.

ON *SONG*

This disputatious and rather brittle play ends with a death instead of the weddings that usually conclude Shakespeare's comedies. Happiness is postponed. But the final words belong to two songs for the cuckoo and the owl, offering a very different debate from the courtly and scholastic disagreements in the rest of the work, between Spring and Winter. It's maybe significant in such an off-centre play that Winter has the last word. The Spring cuckoo with the usual ribald joke threatens the constancy of married love and its daytime cry is a 'word of fear' to all husbands. In this reply the night-owl's hooting is called 'a merry note', ironically. Honest cold replies to treacherous warmth in a kind of anticipation of the later song in *As You Like It*:

> **Here shall he see**
> **No enemy**
> **But winter and rough weather.**

After the complicated banter of the play we are suddenly in a world of everyday realities. The elaborate names of the Dramatis Personae, the King, the Princess, Berowne and the crypto-Biblical Holofernes give way to people from a different stage, as it were, Tom, Joan, Marian and Dick who 'blows his nail'. Apparently this was a popular phrase for idleness; farm workers had little to do at the bleak point of the year. But surely it's also an attempt to warm his hands. Freezing weather makes small comforts matter and the poem makes us conscious of the search for heat, the logs carried into the hall, the roasting of crab-apples to make lamb's-wool and 'greasy Joan', the kitchen-maid, keeping the broth from boiling over ('keel'). In the spring, human behaviour is too hot where winter's search for warmth is more reliable. The delight of such poems lies in the choice of detail, the coughs in church that drown the preacher's moralising ('saws'); the solemn birds sitting out the weather and Marian's raw nose. So pile on those logs (or turn up the central heating), enjoy your lamb's-wool (or make yours a good whisky) and a Merry Christmas to all our readers.

Minted, Practical Poetry for Life,
edited by Brian Nellist

'The banks may not be lending at this moment but what Ruskin called "The King's Treasury" is always open and generous.'

Edited with readers of all tastes in mind, *Minted* is a journey through four centuries of poetry (1500–1900) to encourage further reading and exploration. Read aloud and hear the lines speak to you.

To buy:
Please send a cheque for £6 to The Reader Organisation:

The Reader Organisation (Minted)
The Friary Centre
Bute Street
Liverpool
L5 3LA

See www.thereader.org.uk for more details

THE READING REVOLUTION

DIARIES OF THE READER ORGANISATION

Tales from the Tube
Paul Higgins

I was on my way home on the Piccadilly Line. I had just spent an enjoyable few hours along with fellow Reader chums in the company of Brian Blessed, Eddie Izzard and Stephen Fry at The Criterion. Hilarious!

On the way out I availed myself of a free Vintage copy of *Money* by Martin Amis. I settled down in the carriage amidst a small group of young revellers enlivened by the usual post-chucking-out buzz and opened my new read. One young woman piped up. 'Ooh did you dye that book yourself?' referring to the luminous green that adorned not only the cover of *Money* but also the pages. 'No', I said and returned my eyes to the first page. 'Is it any good?' her mate said. 'I don't know. I have only just got it', I replied and once again looked down. 'What's it about?' the first one said. 'I don't know' I replied once again. By this time I was becoming aware that people beyond myself and this group were looking and listening in.

So I said 'Would you like me to read it to you?' 'Oh. Yes please' they all said in chorus. That way I thought (not totally unselfishly) I could finally make a start before I had to get off at Finsbury Park.

I didn't get beyond the first two paragraphs as the original group announced that they had to get off. I looked up and I could see that this public impromptu reading had created something special. We were all truly together in this carriage, not nursing our smartphones or hooked into our iPods. I could take in my fellow passengers faces as I spread my gaze around and they had taken in the words that I had lifted from the page. We were connected.

How about a bit of P. G. Wodehouse on the 7.20 from Orpington?

A moment in an addiction service group
Jane Davis

There was a new member who joined the group this week, a very thin guy who looked like he'd been a rough sleeper at some time in the past, with bright blue eyes, extremely unshaven and down at heel. He didn't say a word and didn't look at the book. Then, when we stopped to put the kettle on again after an hour, he said in a beautiful soft Scottish accent, 'May I just say something? I am the happiest I have been for a very long time, because I'm sitting here at this table listening to interesting conversation and sharing all this with you'. This looked like a guy you would step over in an alley. Everybody around gulped – we recognised that feeling. 'It's so much better than sitting alone in that little room listening to Radio 4 Extra'. Another group member brought homemade bread for us all to share for breakfast. It was wonderful, one of my best ever moments.

YOUR REGULARS

RED HOT CHILI PINNY

Ian McMillan

I was once in a shop somewhere in Lancashire after I'd been on *Newsnight Review* a couple of days before; a man stared at me like he knew me. He stood beside me just as I was paying for my bag of crisps. 'Do you know Frank?' he said. I shook my head. 'Did you go to school in Ormskirk?' he said. I said 'No.' He paused, thinking. 'Were you on that ferry that was delayed last summer coming into St Malo?' I shook my head again. 'Well, I know you from somewhere' he said, 'Are you a Rochdale fan?'

I didn't know how to reply, and that encapsulates the dilemma of the poet who sometime goes on the television or the radio. Do you say 'You may have seen me on the BBC's flagship late night arts discussion programme, my man!' because inevitably they'll say 'No, I never watch it. Are you sure you weren't on that ferry?' I find it best just to smile and say nothing. Or maybe offer them a crisp.

It's a funny thing, this clashing of the private and the public that happens when they stick a poet in front of a microphone or in the glare of a harsh camera light. It's happened to me a lot, and in the end maybe radio suits poetry more, with its intimacy, the (obvious) fact that you have to concentrate on the sound, and the fact that you don't have to come up with a visual setting for something that's bounded by language. Walk across that snowy field? Stand in front of that photo of miner's banners? Stride through a mocking crowd spouting your deathless verse? I've done 'em all!

For years I was Yorkshire Television's *Investigative Poet*, and the director Dave Beresford and I spent ages trying to work out how to represent poetry on mainstream telly. In the mid-1990s Yorkshire TV were looking for new presenters to make little five-minute films to go on after the news on a programme called *Tonight*, and Dave and I cooked up the idea of making celebratory portraits of Yorkshire life and always finishing them off with a poem by me, delivered to the camera. We made what felt like hundreds of films, on subjects ranging from the fact that the bloke who wrote 'Knees Up Mother Brown' came from Ravensthorpe near Huddersfield to a 'Do-you-remember?' piece about a man who buried himself alive for a year in a field near Barnsley in the 1960s hoping to break the world record for doing so. We made little series of five-minuters looking at buses, at the seven ages of man, at music and performance; in the 1997 Election I put up as the Poetry Candidate and we followed my progress. We graduated to making half-hour films for YTV, on Barnsley FC's rise to the Premier League, and different rituals around death. When the British Council invited me to read poems in Mexico and Argentina Dave went with me and we made half-hour films and repackaged them into five-minute films. And several times during the half-hours, and at the end of the five-minuters, there I was with my little poem.

Now, I have to emphasise that these poems weren't great works of art. They didn't trouble *The Waste Land*. They were quick, hopefully funny, and they rhymed and had strong rhythms because I wanted them to be memorable, in the same way that the work of the early troubadours and bards was memorable because of rhyme and rhythm.

Take the one on Bert Lee, the author of 'Knees Up Mother Brown' for example; we filmed it in the tap room of the pub and as we were a bit late arriving (we were always a bit late arriving) the crowd we'd asked to be there were a bit lively. It didn't matter; I had to do the poem, strolling across the room and out through the door. I had to do it so many times (not my fault,

72

IAN McMILLAN

of course: technical hitches, lights failing, a phone ringing, the landlady's dog howling) that by the time we'd finished all the drinkers knew it too. All together now: 'To me/Bert Lee/Should have been a cockernee/All the Knees Up Mother Brown/Should have come from London town'!

The poems were written hastily, during the filming, in a little reporter's notebook. This meant that I didn't have time to learn them before we had to film them; I did try once or twice but it didn't work, so I just read them from the notebook, and looking back I'm pleased that I did. It gave the viewer an idea of the process, a sense of a poem being 'news that stays news' as Pound said, and it suggested that a poet could be a public person, someone like a politician or a journalist or a comedian that you could turn to to get a take on what's happening around you and how it could be informed by what's happened before and suggest what might happen in the future.

Mind you, sometimes your TV appearances are out of your control. I once appeared on a special *Ready Steady Cook* for National Poetry Day with the great Sophie Hannah and, despite setting fire to some kitchen roll, I won. Sophie, coming second (well, losing) got a hamper and I got a hundred quid in cash and my Red Pepper Pinny. When you don't drink and you have a drink it's a disaster, as J. P. Sartre said that time. I got on the train at King's Cross and began to spend a large amount of the cash on beer. I bought drinks for baffled businessmen from Peterborough and grateful students on their way home to Darlington. I said, slurring my words 'I've been on *Ready Steady Cook* you know!' and to prove it I put the pinny on. People applauded and I bought them more beer. 'I'm a poet and I've been on *Ready Steady Cook*!' I shouted. I sat in a seat and slumped. I nodded off. I dribbled down the pinny. Suddenly a voice on the tannoy said 'Next stop Doncaster' and I ran from the train, still wearing the pinny. A man I knew slightly came up and said 'You've been on *Ready Steady Cook*!' How on earth did he know?

One more time: 'To me/Bert Lee/Should have been a cockernee…'

THE READING REVOLUTION

CREATIVE TRANSLATIONS

Casi Dylan

Between thought and expression lies a lifetime.
'Some Kind of Love', The Velvet Underground

W e're in Tŷ Newydd on the Llŷn Peninsula, and I'm standing between two flipcharts with a poem in my hand. Of the thirteen people that sit facing me, poem also in their hands, I know that one cannot understand me. That's my colleague Clare. Clare is here with me as a course leader, but as this is the first bi-lingual Read to Lead – Welsh and English – and as she does not speak Welsh, she sits with us, listening, participating as much as is possible without following the conversation. Tŷ Newydd itself seems to have been designed with reading aloud in mind. It was Lloyd George's home before it became the National Writer's Centre for Wales; the room above our heads was where he entertained and practiced his speeches – the modest ceiling domed so as to boost the acoustics. But good acoustics can do little to assist our Clare as we turn back to the poem, R. Williams Parry's astounding sonnet 'Dinas Noddfa', which begins:

Pan yrr y Sêr eu cryndod drwy dy waed
Gan siglo dy gredoau megis dail;
Pan brofo'r Nos y pridd o'r hwn y'th wnaed,
A'i hofn yn chwilio'th sylwedd hyd i'th sail;

Clumsily we try to translate between us. 'It's called "The Fort of Refuge", or maybe "The City of Sanctuary". It sort of goes like: "When the Stars send their awe through your blood / And shake your beliefs as if they were leaves;/ When the Night tests the clay of which you're made, / And its fear searches your substance to its foundation."' We're not up to much really, bashfully aware of the scale of poetry lost. And yet for the time being, it is not this process of translation that concerns us. Because I am standing between two flipcharts to run an exercise on the practice of preparing the use of your literature in a shared reading group. In the course pack the exercise is called 'Preparing Your Material' but through repeated practice it's coming to be called 'Creative Translations'.

The premise is simple. On one flipchart we note individual responses to the poem – anything that strikes you, moves you, intrigues you as a reader. With the same freedom that is extended to any member of a shared reading group, responses – opinions – come easily, the page fills up quickly. Experienced readers are fluent in this process, and quicker to build meaning from what they read: 'It's about a kind of primal terror this poem, isn't it? Those dark nights of the soul where even the very basis of your life seems under scrutiny.' 'There is hope here though, sanctuary – just look at the title – but it's a sanctuary that you must build for yourself.' 'I do like that sentiment – "Yn Arglwydd dy ddiddymdra" – Lord of your nothingness – but I'm not sure I like the religious tone of it.' Comments from greyer areas are sometimes more quietly voiced: 'It feels enormous, this, but I think I like it.'

And so on to the second flipchart, where the group – all working to become shared reading practitioners – is asked to make use of these personal impressions in order to design possible questions or prompts that they could use when facilitating a group of their own. That is, 'Now that you've had all these thoughts about the poem, give me the very words that will come

CASI DYLAN

out of your mouth when leading a group'. This time the page takes longer to fill. It becomes clear very quickly that opinions by themselves no longer cut it on Flipchart Two, phrases that begin with 'This poem is about...' are seen as conversation killers when voiced by the group leader (or any group member come to that). So too any hint of cynicism, disengagement. By asking future practitioners to move away from assertions about what they read, the process demands the question: what is there left to be said?

In part, the translation element of this exercise is the practice of moving away from easy fluency to useful inarticulacy. The time spent exploring in between the flipcharts reveals that it's the simplest questions that are most enabling: 'Where are we here, do you think?', 'What's your sense of what's happening?', 'Does it remind you of anything?' Expression itself need not reflect the complexity of the impression the literature has inspired. We also find voicing the thoughts from greyer areas works well when offered out to the group: 'It feels enormous, this poem, but I think I like it' belongs to that useful, shady area prior to thought and opinion.

Mari is uncomfortable with this process. 'Darnio', that's her accusation, literally 'to break into bits'. In one sense she is right, but rather than breaking down the poem, we're working with the process of forming your thoughts in relation to the poem, how you come to think what you think. The flipcharts and the space between are the visualisation and the holding steady of a process that must happen at synaptic speed with every word you read: calling upon personal experience to inform understanding. It can be an uncomfortable feeling making yourself aware of this process, not least because one of the great joys of reading is to come across a voice in books that is so perfectly itself that it seems ungracious to question it. But in running shared reading groups it is your role not only to have a firm grasp of the literature you're working with, but a grasp on how to re-create that process of coming-to-understanding. In order to achieve this it's as if you've got to go back somewhere behind your own thoughts, to trace how you got there. Inevitably, what lies behind the impression are the tiny details of the writing itself, lodged so quickly away in the forming of an idea that they are barely noticed in the process.

The constant challenge for the group leader is to find 'the way in' that best serves this story, this poem, this group. Whilst anyone who has led groups in any capacity will know the importance of an open question, offering out 'What's this poem about, then?' – even when softened with genuine curiosity of tone and intention – is not good enough: too baggy, too open, too reliant on the presumption that the group will think the poem 'about' anything at all! Project workers who facilitate many groups every week will certainly have built a store of questions that tend to work in a variety of settings, but these will be crafted to draw attention to specifics in the writing, not generalities. 'Shall we read that one again?' is always a necessary question, establishing the literature as the focus of attention. 'Is there anything that stands out for you?' allows group members to become conscious of what they've noticed, to pick a starting point for themselves from which the facilitator can then navigate the session. Every piece that you bring to the group will require a different way in, be it through time, place, person: it is the facilitator's work to take notice and to make use of these to ground the group in the specificity of the piece.

I recently ran a training session with a group of Care Assistants in Glasgow, and was struck by how attuned they were to this process of recreating the reality of what the literature was offering them. We went through how we might prepare John Masefield's 'Sea Fever' for a group of their residents, and they immediately latched onto the poem's tangibles, its sensations: 'That struck me as a beautiful line, Peggy: "And all I ask is a windy day with the white clouds flying". I wonder, have you ever been down to the sea on a windy day?' It was wonderful to see the kindness, sincerity and imagination that informed their questions. Wonderful too, their understanding of how it is sometimes necessary to go out of the literary world of the poem to come back into it again, reinforced with personal experience. Regained. Little wonder perhaps, in a workplace so concerned with reinforcing the reality of a life lived through a 'grey mist' of its own.

But it is not only in such settings that a literal, grounded language can be used to channel a literary thought. To a greater and lesser extent, it's true of every group. In another course, this time in London, a group of trainees went through the creative translation of Elizabeth Jennings' 'Delay':

> **The radiance of that star that leans on me**
> **Was shining years ago. The light that now**
> **Glitters up there my eye may never see,**
> **And so the time lag teases me with how**
>
> **Love that loves now may not reach me until**
> **Its first desire is spent. The star's impulse**
> **Must wait for eyes to claim it beautiful**
> **And love arrived may find us somewhere else.**

In a poem that seems to be about the very sensation of missing something, the space in-between things, there is a temptation to skip straight to abstraction, generalisations. But, as with 'Dinas Noddfa', the cosmic scale is complemented and understood through a human measure, one used directly to serve the other. And so once more, from first impressions we search out the human detail. From 'That's scientifically true isn't it? Starlight doesn't reach us until the star has collapsed' we reach back for 'When did you last look up at the stars?' From '"The star's impulse / Must wait for eyes to claim it beautiful" – that's how I hold on to this poem' we come back to 'Is there a line, a word, a picture that stands out for you?' From 'I find this such a sad poem', we work through it together, and find the emotion held not so much in the words 'love' or 'desire' as those counterpoints in time: the difference between 'now' and 'now', 'until', 'may never', 'may find'. That blank space at the poem's heart.

It's the span of that gap that demands the practice of 'creative translation'. The translation between literary and literal seems to be one element of the huge effort of adaptation that is required to connect with any other human being. There is a passage from *Middlemarch* that we have read on almost every Read to Lead course to date. It's taken from Dorothea and Casaubon's honeymoon in Rome, where it seems that Dorothea's expectations of marriage do not tally with the reality of the man who is her husband. The couple have had their first marital disagreement:

> **Dorothea remembered it to the last with the vividness with which we all remember epochs in our experience when some dear expectation dies, or some new motive is born. Today she had begun to see that she had been under a wild illusion in expecting a response to her feeling from Mr. Casaubon, and she had felt the waking of a presentiment that there might be a sad consciousness in his life which made as great a need on his side as on her own.**
>
> **We are all of us born in moral stupidity, taking the world as an udder to feed our supreme selves: Dorothea had early begun to emerge from that stupidity, but yet it had been easier to her to imagine how she would devote herself to Mr. Casaubon, and become wise and strong in his strength and wisdom, than to conceive with that distinctness which is no longer reflection but feeling – an idea wrought back to the directness of sense, like the solidity of objects – that he had an equivalent centre of self, whence the lights and shadows must always fall with a certain difference.**

The claim of 'moral stupidity' at the beginning of the second paragraph kicks out at you, challenges you to think out of the specificities of a Victorian couple into the undeniable, indelible 'need' to see beyond ourselves, to imaginatively conceive of every other person as an 'equivalent centre of self.' I love the precision of that combination of 'equivalent' and 'a certain difference'. And again, it's in the process of working backwards, back past thought and 'reflection' to the solidity of 'feeling – an idea wrought back to the directness of sense' that brings out the reality not only of Casaubon's existence, but Dorothea's own. She must register, and register again and again, the reality of that sense, even if it is felt only as 'the waking of a presentiment that there might be...' Like the grey areas in which our original intimations of the literature are found, that sense seems to be reaching out from the thing that matters most, and offers the opportunity to build a creative language in the distance between us.

THE READING REVOLUTION

SOUND AND VISION

Damian Taylor

When first asked, as part of my role as Reader-in-Residence at Greater Manchester West Mental Health Trust, to set up a Get Into Reading group at the John Denmark Unit I felt a good deal more trepidation than usual. The reason for this being that the JDU is the National Centre for Mental Health and Deafness. It provides care for people who are deaf and have severe and enduring mental illness. Would it be possible to take the Get Into Reading model, which relies so heavily on reading aloud, and adapt it for use here? How exactly would I go about translating literature into Sign?

Over the course of several months, I visited the unit and met with ward staff and service users, while also learning about Deaf culture and attempting to comprehend the complexity of British Sign Language (BSL). It became increasingly clear that a professional British Sign Language interpreter would be required to help translate the words from the page into Sign, and then to interpret group members' responses into spoken English.

The group meets once a week. We sit around the table and drink tea like any other reading group. As some participants have limited hearing or are capable of lip reading I still read the poem aloud whilst the interpreter (Chris) simultaneously signs the poem. The poem is 'read' not so much from the written page (although all group members are provided with a paper copy) but from the signs which flicker from the hands of the interpreter.

BSL is the natural language of the Deaf in the UK. It is a visual-gestural system as opposed to the verbal-auditory system of spoken English. The signer uses both hands to produce sign shapes which are then interpreted or read by the audience. It is a mistake to think of BSL as merely miming actions or using pictorial gestures to symbolise objects or words. While some signs do indeed mirror everyday gestures (such as pointing to the wrist to sign TIME), BSL is a complex language with its own syntax and grammar, and completely different to that of English.

Although it can be useful to think of a sign as being equivalent to a word, this isn't strictly true. A single sign, provided by the shape of the hands is in essence 'the meaning', but meaning can be modified by using information carried by the head, face and body to indicate the size, shape, and movement of an object, or to give an object a temporal location in the past, present or future. Furthermore, this information can be transmitted simultaneously. A deaf person can perform a sign in a moment that will take an interpreter several seconds and spoken sentences to spell out. It is therefore not possible to translate English into BSL on a word-by-word basis as the linear structures of English do not make for effective signs.

Whilst spoken English uses a subject–verb–object order, BSL is structured as topic–comment. For example, the sentence 'I drove the car' would be translated in BSL as CAR – ME – DRIVE. Alongside the change in word order, you will also notice that the verb drive is signed in the present tense; this is because the tense of a sign is suggested by its position in relation to the rest of the body, and not by the sign itself.

The use of facial expression and body language can also be used to demonstrate what type of car you were driving, a rickety old wreck or sports car, and can also convey if the drive was invigorating, tiring, boring, or exciting. The only limit to how many ways a sign can be modified is the signer's knowledge-base, how much they know about any given object or action.

Some service users at the John Denmark Unit have had limited life experience, whether due to their illness, or the effect of being in long-term care, and because of this small knowledge-base, they are inclined to interpret the meaning of BSL in a concrete way. Consequently, the interpreter must avoid providing literal translations of the poems and, instead, employ a certain level of creative initiative.

For example, when you hear the word 'starfish' the image which appears in the mind's eye is that of a five-fingered sea creature. The mind does not interpret each morpheme individually, first picturing a star and then a fish, then attempt to place the two meanings together. You bring all your knowledge about starfish, the sea, and any number of other associations drawn from memory and feeling to give meaning to the word.

A literal translation of the word starfish into BSL would be broken down into the individual morphemes and so would be signed using STAR, as in the celestial body, and the sign FISH. Without the knowledge-base of what a starfish actually is, group members are likely to wonder what a fish is doing in outer space. To overcome this, images and props are used to help ground the sign and to avoid unnecessary qualification: 'It is like a star in the sky, but it isn't, it is a fish, but it doesn't look like a fish, it is shaped like a star', *ad infinitum*.

Poetry can provide a framework which encourages the use of the reader's existing knowledge-base while also encouraging cognitive leaps and fresh connections. When poetry is translated into BSL, the group members are not receiving the *words* of the poem but the *meaning*. To sign individual signs in an attempt to translate the words on the page would be equivalent to reading the words out in a stilted monotone. If you did this, it could not be denied that you had read the poem, but you would not have given the words their shades of meaning. The use of tone, emphasis, and our own thoughts and feelings add additional meaning when we read aloud. Sign itself is less word-based and relies heavily upon the signer's creative expression to transfer not just the words but the meaning.

When reading the following lines from the poem 'A Cup of Tea': 'When the world is all at odds / And the mind is all at sea', connections are made between the external world in turmoil and the internal emotional experience of feeling isolated and adrift.

Translated into BSL this would appear WORLD – CONFUSED – MIND – SEA. At first glance the translation of BSL into written English may appear drained of poetic language; the four words sound dead and heavy. But if you were to observe the above lines signed, this is what you would see: First two hands moving around an invisible globe, working from the North Pole to the South, the hands are then brought up together and pause in front of the chest, and then move up and around over the front of the head, before suddenly springing forward in rough waves.

I had been worried that group members would sit and wonder how on earth your mind could take a boat trip. However, as soon as the interpreter signed this line, a group member suddenly began to respond, signing 'When I feel like that I want to pull my head off.'

The act of signing a poem is the act of making the meaning of that poem *in the moment*, translating the meaning through your own body rather than just saying what the words are. This lifting of the poem off the page allows each group member to access their own knowledge-base of the world, not just of the physical world but also their own inner emotional geography.

Literature can help to fill the void in our knowledge-bases, either by providing the chance to explore new worlds or ideas, or by giving names to those worlds and ideas already experienced but perhaps not recognised or expressed. Even if a sign or word is unfamiliar to a group member the act of reading aloud, of signing or saying the word enables a meaning to be created. When we read a poem we interpret the shape of each individual word or sign – not just in terms of its physical shape on the page, but also its hidden internal shape, which is revealed as the words pass through a living thing. Each reading is an act of translation, from the symbols on the page to thoughts in the mind, the poem becomes the experience, and we find that while not understanding a line of Shakespeare we are simultaneously able to know, deeply, what it means.

The Reader Organisation has received funding from the D'Oyly Carte Charitable Trust to enable professional BSL translation at the JDU.

YOUR REGULARS

'THIS IS FOR EVERYONE'
THE MAKING OF THE OLYMPIC OPENING CEREMONY

Jane Davis

The Reader Organisation is in year two of a project to develop a culture of reading for pleasure amongst student teachers at Liverpool Hope University. Two rather different men put the idea into my head. One – the obvious one – was author, patron of our charity, and this year's *Guardian* Children's Fiction Prize winner, Frank Cottrell Boyce. He told me, 'We've got to do something about teachers. I'm going into primary schools and doing lovely events with the kids, and then sitting in staff rooms talking with the teachers who invited me there but who don't read themselves'. The second influence was Rod Holmes, the man who led the immense Liverpool One Development Project. He had agreed to meet for an hour to give me some business advice. I described what we do and the first thing he said was 'teachers'. When I looked blank, he expanded, 'They are the multiplier.'

If a primary school teacher teaches 30 children each year for 35 years they have the potential for a direct and profound influence on about 1000 children. At Liverpool Hope we are working with 175 student teachers this year: that is potentially 175,000 profound influences. Yes indeed, they are multipliers.

So when Professor Gerald Pillay, the Vice-chancellor at Hope contacted me to talk about setting up a project within the University I responded at once. He had the guts to admit what many in Higher Education are still choking on: most students don't read. The minority of students who do are mostly reading what's popular: J. K. Rowling, Andy McNab or *The Hunger Games*. This is not just about taste and alternative media; it's also about confidence and consumerism. The books people read are easy to sell in large numbers and easy to consume. Not Milton, not Austen, not Shakespeare.

But when Frank asked Danny Boyle to come to Hope to talk to the students about why reading matters, suddenly it seemed Milton, Jane Austen, William Blake, John Cooper-Clarke and Paul Farley were in everyone's interest. Frank was the writer in Boyle's Olympics opening ceremony team, and they have also worked together on several films.

Do you remember that great moment in the ceremony when Sir Tim Berners-Lee was revealed sitting at a keyboard and behind him was a message in lights: 'This is for everyone'. I thought of that as Frank got Danny talking about how they had created the ceremony. They constructed it out of everything they loved about Britain, and it was made to draw on what we, 'everyone', have in common. I met Frank and Danny in the Hope car-park that darkening October evening and, while shaking hands with Danny, said 'Thank you for making me feel patriotic for the first time'. It turns out thousands of people have been saying exactly the same thing to him. That is not an accident, that is a *result*.

So this is how you put together an Olympic opening ceremony. Danny told the student teachers:

> **We had a room where we'd meet every day, for nine months. We had the most amazing job. We asked ourselves three questions: 'Where do we come from?', 'What are we?' and 'Where do we hope to be?' or *'What do we hope to be?'* We asked ourselves those three questions and we sat round and talked about that.**

Comparing it to the transformation of a workaday primary school classroom into a fantastic 'treat place', Frank added:

> **We were sticking our favourite things on the wall; favourite quotations; reading each other bits and things; finding poems; bits of films; bits of music, and putting this big scrapbook together of stuff that we loved.**

They stood at the front of the hall, like ordinary guys in jeans and casual shirts, ignoring the chairs set out for them, so everyone at the back could see, and began to speak to each other, and eventually to us, in a natural, memory-jogging sort of workmate way. Frank read a section from Humphrey Jennings' book, *Pandaemonium*. He had given a copy of *Pandaemonium* to Danny as a Christmas present one year. 'Have you read it yet?' he said he kept asking. He had bought it second-hand before the new reprint and it cost a lot. Danny hadn't read it. Frank kept asking, and finally had to demand, 'Have you read it yet? *It cost me £50!*' But the book went on to become such an inspiration that the opening sequence, in which huge furnaces and chimneys rose from the ground of the stadium, was named after it. At the end of the talk, Frank gave me a copy of new edition of the book, for which he has written the introduction, signed by both of them, to be used as part of the Hope Readers project.

Frank and Danny – and the rest of their creative team – were readers but not *just* readers of books, as Danny was keen to point out. Danny and Frank are Northerners, working class, state educated – like half the country, then – but they were lovers of music, readers of magazines, of cartoons, watchers of films, fans of *The Wire*. They were people, in others words, who liked or loved particular things, who had obsessions, passions, crazy deep interests in things with no apparent meaning. A lot of us are made up of this scattered stuff. Danny spoke about how little a random group of people seem to have in common:

As a director, when you direct actors in a play, you have this exercise. When they first come together it can be a bit intimidating and you need exercises to break the ice. You do this one exercise called 'common culture': I would break you into a group of about ten, and you have to come back within five minutes and present to the other groups as much common culture that you all know. The only stipulation is that all ten of you must know it – *must* know it – and you've got to present it back to us. And it's terrible. What we all have in common is really thin. It boils down, usually, to the National

**Anthem and a bit at the start of 'Our Father' – a prayer.
It's really thin, what we all know together.**

That was a creative problem for the Opening Ceremony team.
But, Frank went on to say, there are many things we've *forgotten*.
'We do share stuff, but you've forgotten', he said, and I had a
shiver at that moment, because it felt like a moment from Doris
Lessing's novel, *Shikasta*. Danny explained how this had fed into
the idea of the ceremony:

**One of the hidden themes of our opening ceremony is
that there is a thumbprint of culture that is in you...
there are things that are hidden in our culture that you
don't realise yet and you'll find them, or they'll find you.**

Most of us haven't read *Frankenstein* by Mary Shelley, but the
book has so much power as an act of imagination that it has
passed into common currency. People don't realise when they
see Colin Clive or Benedict Cumberbatch playing Frankenstein
that they are accessing something imagined by an 18-year-old
girl. It was one of the key books behind the ceremony:

Frankenstein **is part of the way we think. When science
comes up with something new like GM crops, there's
always that debate: 'Is this bad? Is it Frankenstein?' –
that idea that you create a monster that destroys you.
It's part of the way we think about the world, and
part of our imaginative vocabulary and our emotional
vocabulary, but it was made up by writers.**

(Frank Cottrell Boyce)

I first met Frank when we chose his novel, *Millions*, as our
Liverpool Reads book in 2005. I'd read the novel, in the lovely
original hardback edition with the golden cover, with my son
Ben, the summer he left school. At 18, anyone might have
thought he was too old for *Millions*, but no – and neither was I.
It is a wonderful book, profound and ordinary and funny, which
is exactly what Frank is absolutely brilliant at doing. And there's
the rub. Danny Boyle and Frank Cottrell Boyce were there to

urge this huge audience of students not just to read to but to believe, to feel, to care, to *love* things. Collect stuff, Danny urged, showing his multi-coloured notebook. Write things down, notice them – look! He flipped it open and showed us his notes. Scraps of songs, bits of billboard adverts and passages from books and poems. The pair spoke about the necessity of putting stuff into your head if you want your imagination to bring stuff out:

You can only give back what you are given, in one form or another: you feel impelled to pass on what you love. And that is why teaching and being an educator is a position of such massive privilege.

(Danny Boyle)

This is the multiplier effect. It was what comes from that – from *believing* – that gave the ceremony the funny, generous, small-scale, magnificent feeling that I recognised as *my* country. It was knowing and witty but it was never cynical or merely clever. Danny Boyle said what might seem to some a strange thing; 'I don't believe in God but I believe in the people who do – this is their show, they really are the best of us'. Paraphrasing G. K. Chesterton, Frank stressed:

The world is not perishing for lack of wonders. The world is perishing for lack of wonder. It's that thing of making you look at the world that's around you and making you own it, and making you see that it is amazing. I hope that's what we did with the ceremony. When people say, 'it made me feel patriotic', what we did was represent the culture that we all live in and say, 'Look, it's amazing. You just forgot. You just forgot to *notice* that you're amazing; that this is an amazing place.

There were risks too in this way of showing Britain to the world and to itself. 'You were brave,' Frank said to Danny, and explained to the audience how the reputation of a film-maker is his only currency. 'You risked your reputation if it had flopped.'

Danny talked about how the makers of TV programmes are cowed by what people will think or say about them. Standards of creativity drop 'because people are afraid of the *Daily Mail*'. But he had taken a decision early on to go with what they, the creators believed, and to believe in it wholeheartedly and absolutely. People might not like it but they would all recognise it had a stamp of integrity, of authenticity. It didn't matter if some didn't know the Sex Pistols, or if they didn't get the references to Blake. It *did* matter that the team shared all the things they loved, and that they could imagine other people would love them too: the Queen, James Bond, corgis. Danny then read Paul Farley's 'A Poem for The Queen'. Frank, ever-mindful of his audiences, offered to raise his hand when the swear words came, so people of a nervous disposition, or just young, like his own children in the audience, could close their ears. The poem, which refers to the Queen 'waking up / in the blue silence of seven hundred rooms' was part of the inspiration for the sequence with James Bond and the Queen at Buckingham Palace and Danny said:

I would encourage the Queen to read. Because if there is anything that could tell her, when she wakes up in that massive house with seven hundred rooms, that she is not alone – it would be in a book!

During the conversation, Danny quoted C. S. Lewis's words, 'We read to know that we are not alone'.

As they spoke in their easy, bantering way I remembered what I had loved in the ceremony: the hammering Pandemonium of *Paradise Lost*, the Blakean furnaces heating metal into heavenly golden rings. That it was a literary ceremony! It was all about books! Children's books, Peter Pan, Mary Poppins, Harry Potter. And the great books – *The Tempest*, Jane Austen, Dickens. The Olympic Cauldron was out of Dante's *Paradiso*, surely, where the whole of everything comes together in one enormous fire?

I saw gathered there in the depths of it,
Bound up by love into a single volume,
All the leaves scattered through the Universe;
Substance and accidents and their relations,
But yet fused together in such a manner
That what I am talking of is a simple light.

POETRY

MELISSA LEE-HOUGHTON

Mummy Wakes at Dawn

She would fall asleep each night,
on the bus ride home, the chugging of the engine
and her feet lolling over the edge of the seat.
I would look at her reflection in the window
as though looking at someone else's daughter.
I'd have to wake her,
carrying her to the shop
for milk and bread and tobacco
and have her cry all the way home,
only to watch her play with her food and
look at me as though I was someone else's mother.
Her eyes would glaze over, she looked like
one of those ceramic dolls old women keep in their houses.
I'd put her to bed in a cold room
where she'd wake and clamber down to the floor
with her little pillow and bunch up tight there
by the foot of her bed.
Often, I would find myself getting in her bed
to sleep for the night. I worried about her being alone –
I worried about myself. I prayed
and crossed my heart
for the sun rising above the terraced roofs
coming in quickly, without sleep to hold me
and I would wait for dawn to break, my hands

under my pillow, clasped.
A new day.
Just the same as the last one,
faded like old peroxide
and stubborn.
I would wake her, so softly,
and she would pull and tease at my hair and we could
see our breath in the early morning,
she'd say, 'smoke.' I'd light a cigarette
by the back door while she picked at her toast.
We'd be thinking of the people we missed most.
Sometimes, she just wouldn't make eye contact.
Sometimes, I just wouldn't try.

YOUR REGULARS

ASK THE READER

Brian Nellist

Q After all the fuss about Dickens this year it was a relief to see that The Reader has preserved a dignified silence, despite one or two references in passing. As a journal with serious interests how could you join in the adulation of that gallimaufry of pantomime and journalism with grotesques in place of characters, maudlin sentiment (all those dead children) in place of real feeling and women who are passive angels or absurd harridans?

A Funny you should complain about journalism and angels in the same breath! His exaggeration is the pressure put upon realism by his extravagant imagination. The last of his Christmas Books is called *The Haunted Man*, the story of a man so overwhelmed by a bitter past that he surrenders memory altogether to free himself and finds in that condition an even greater curse. But I don't want to appeal to biography because it's what the novels mean to the reader that matters more than how they illumine Dickens. You call his characters grotesques because you isolate them from the context of the whole vision that constitutes the individual novel. You may protest that Mr Murdstone in *David Copperfield* is a caricature of the cruel Evangelical step-father but he exists alongside David's other adopted 'father', Mr Dick, an idiot to the likes of the Murdstones, who through his native kindness understands the marriage of Dr and Mrs Strong and can mend it where they would bring only dismissive contempt. Except of course that in the adopted home it's Betsey Trotwood who is the strong, managing figure and Dick who is the unobtrusive presence, always consulted about matters of the heart. Steerforth excuses his predatoriness in advance to David of all people with the excuse that he's lacked a guiding father. What do strength and weakness mean in the novel? Who is more apparently 'grotesque' than Betsey herself at the start storming out of the house because her sister-in-law has failed to produce a girl, or her manic cries of 'Donkeys, donkeys' when her sacred turf is invaded. Yet she is warmed into magnificent humanity by her love for David and we hear no more about intrusive hooves. Dickens, like a dramatist, doesn't explain the psychological structure in the novels but leaves the reader to apprehend them. No character might seem more overdrawn than Mrs Gamp, however funny the result, but the nursing that's undertaken for money contrasts with the other contracted nurse, Mary Graham, who offers old Martin Chuzzlewit patience and love, a love which extends to his grandson, young Martin. Wretched Sairey Gamp can find self-valuation only by inventing Mrs Harris, to preserve whom she's prepared to sacrifice her only real associate Betsey Prig. In a novel so concerned with delusion it's the perceptiveness that moves the reader as much as the humour.

You can never take Dickens' own remarks about his work at face value but, as Lawrence said, trust the tale and not the teller; he can't afford to enquire too intimately about the source of his inspiration. After 'selfishness' in *Martin Chuzzlewit*, he would analyse 'pride' in *Dombey and Son*, which tells us very little. Mr Dombey is the victim of the firm which casts a kind of glory about him that stifles all his feelings (as ancestry, almost, does with Dedlock in *Bleak House*). But the 'pride' of Edith, the second Mrs Dombey, is a resentment at being turned into a mere object in the marriage market which feeds a voluble rhetoric that drowns the husband who scarcely puts two words together. They are both in a sense stagey characters but that is the author's perceptiveness not his failure.

I mention *Dombey* because you are thinking, I bet, of the death of little Paul Dombey, one of Dicken's fey kids. Death is important to him not because of a morbid streak but because it challenges as no other fact can the values by which we live. Children die in his novels because in a sense they have no place in the order of the world as he has envisioned it. Little Nell herself has fled so many dangers that her death becomes only the final flight. What you call journalism, the exposure of workhouses, Yorkshire schools, factories and mines are for him instances of the 'mind-forged manacles' that the world fastens on the individual. His vision is closer to Blake than to the *Daily Express* or even the *Guardian*. In a world dominated by men his women must either become male or, like the children, become 'passive angels', witnesses against the oppression of tenderness and pity. A member of a CE class drew my attention the other day to an apparently awkward passage about the sufferings of Mercy Pecksniff with her brutal husband, Jonas Chuzzlewit:

> **Oh woman, God beloved in old Jerusalem! The best among us need deal lightly with thy faults, if only for the punishment thy nature will endure, in bearing heavy evidence against us on the Day of Judgement.**

The 'we' and 'us' is the male sex, of course, that has all the power and women will suffer on Doomsday because despite their loving natures they will have to tell the truth on that occasion against even those they love. Oh yes, but that's easy to say, you will reply, for a man who was eventually to desert his wife. But the Divine imperatives are not a casual add-on for Dickens; they lie at the centre of his vision, a word I keep using, I know, because he is above all a visionary writer. A great comic novelist he undoubtedly is but he is also a disconcertingly serious man.

YOUR RECOMMENDATIONS

BOOKS ABOUT...

Angela Macmillan

The collection this time has no real theme. They are simply books I have enjoyed recently and want to pass on. Mostly I read them on holiday in the USA so you will notice an American bias. American paperbacks are such a joy to handle, almost worth the extra expense just to have a softback that does not either spring shut or crack when you try and open it wider than a couple of inches.

Charles Dickens, *Barnaby Rudge* (1841)
Vintage Classics ISBN-13: 978-0099540847

'I don't invent it – really do not – but see it and write it down', said Dickens and when you read the scenes that describe London during the Gordon Riots of 1780, and the burning of Newgate Prison, you must believe him. The intensity of his vision puts you as reader in the midst of the roaring, raging mob and the experience is electrifying. Some of his characters are oddly sketchy and the structure is a little mismanaged – it's not mature Dickens, but it is always engrossing and I can't imagine why I had not read it before or why it has not been adapted for film or television. The outrageous raven, Grip, must be literature's best bird.

Kevin Powers, *The Yellow Birds* (2012)
Sceptre ISBN-13: 978-1444756128

When Kevin Powers came back from serving in the United States Army in Iraq, the question he was most asked was, 'what was it like?' Powers is a poet and this fine, lyric novel is his best attempt at an answer to that essentially unanswerable question. It is about the terrible impact of combat upon a boy from Virginia and powerfully reinforces what we must already know by now, that war kills those who fight it. If not by bullets and bombs, by breaking the mind, spoiling the past and damaging the future. It is an old story, newly told for the twenty-first century and deserves to be widely read.

Meg Wolitzer, *The Wife* (2003)
Vintage ISBN-13: 978-0099478195

The novel covers a period in America from the 1950s to the millennium. Narrated by Joan Castleman, it is the story of the choices and compromises in her forty-year marriage to prizewinning novelist Joe; a story that begins at the moment she decides to leave him. It is about individual identity and what happens to that in the privacy of a marriage full of paradox – love and hate, betrayal and loyalty, independence and dependence, clarity and self-deception. It is angry and bitter and funny; not unlike reading Philip Roth. Towards the end Joan reflects that she has probably been a good wife, which made me think hard about the role of 'wife' and in particular how difficult it must have been to live this role over a period which saw such radical changes in political, economic and social rights for women.

Colum McCann, *Let the Great World Spin* **(2010)**
Bloomsbury ISBN-13: 978-1408801185

In 1974, a man set a tightrope between the top of the almost completed twin towers of The World Trade Centre and walked across. Colum McCann zooms in on a handful of the 9 million lives on the streets of New York below; lives crossing and interconnecting in ways they might never come to know. Wonderfully life-affirming, this book takes a clear-eyed look up at the heavens and down in the gutter. It is not a book about 9/11 but it is impossible to talk of the towers without thinking of their destruction and somehow, even though McCann never presses the point, the image of the walker inching forward into the clouds, above all the grief and despair down below, is like a prevailing light throughout the book: a reason to look up. I can't do justice to this terrifically ambitious novel in a few lines; suffice it to say it is one of the few books I have finished and begun again straight away.

Andrew Greig, *At the Loch of the Green Corrie* **(2011)**
Quercus ISBN-13: 978-0857381361

Shortly before his death, the Scottish poet Norman McCaig suggested to his friend Andrew Greig, that he fish for him in *The Loch of the Green Corrie*. Some years later, in the company of two good friends, Greig went in search of the Loch. Their days in Assynt are filled with the emotive landscape, their shared past, their affection for each other, their plans for the future and of course, fishing. There is nothing trivial here. Greig reflects on the history and geology of Scotland, the meaning of whisky, the importance of kinship and, recovering from serious illness – on what it means to be alive. For a longer review see http://threaderonline.co.uk/2012/08/15/recommended-read/

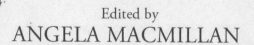

Edited by
ANGELA MACMILLAN

A Little,
ALOUD
for children

An anthology of poems and stories
to share aloud

Financial Times
Book of the Year
for Children

'An absolutely
impeccable
anthology'

£9.99 RRP

Or £5.99 (+ p&p)
from www.
thereader.org.uk

With a foreword by
MICHAEL MORPURGO

A LITTLE *MORE* ALOUD

R. L. STEVENSON,

THE STRANGE CASE OF DR JEKYLL AND MR HYDE

Selected by Angela Macmillan

Most people know something of this story even if they have never actually read Stevenson's novella. Our extract comes very near the beginning and is perfect for reading aloud. Mr Utterson, a lawyer, and his friend Enfield are taking an evening walk through the streets of Edinburgh when they come upon a sinister looking doorway.

Chapter I.

'Did you ever remark that door?' … 'It is connected in my mind, with a very odd story.'

'Indeed?' said Mr. Utterson, with a slight change of voice, 'and what was that?'

'Well, it was this way,' returned Mr. Enfield: 'I was coming home from some place at the end of the world, about three o'clock of a black winter morning, and my way lay through a part of town where there was literally nothing to be seen but lamps. Street after street and all the folks asleep – street after street, all lighted up as if for a procession and all as empty as a church – till at last I got into that state of mind when a man listens and listens and begins to long for the sight of a policeman. All at once, I saw two figures: one a little man who was stumping along eastward at a good walk, and the other a girl of maybe eight or ten who was running as hard as she was able down a cross street. Well, sir, the two ran into one another naturally enough at the corner; and then came the horrible part of the thing; for the man trampled calmly over the child's body and left her screaming on the ground. It sounds nothing to hear, but it was hellish to see. It wasn't like a man; it was like some damned Juggernaut. I gave a view halloa, took to my heels, collared my gentleman, and brought him back to where there was already quite a group about the screaming child. He was perfectly cool and made no resistance, but gave me one look, so ugly that it brought out the sweat on me like running. The people who had turned out were the girl's own family; and pretty soon, the doctor, for whom she had been sent, put in his appearance. Well, the child was not much the worse, more frightened, according to the Sawbones; and there you might have supposed would be an end to it. But there was one curious circumstance. I had taken a loathing to my gentleman at first sight. So had the child's family, which was only natural. But the doctor's case was what struck me. He was the usual cut and dry apothecary, of no particular age and colour, with a strong Edinburgh accent, and about as emotional as a bagpipe. Well, sir, he was like the rest of us; every time he looked at my prisoner, I saw that Sawbones turned sick and white with desire to kill him. I knew what was in his mind, just as he knew what was in mine; and killing being out of the question, we did the next best. We told the man we could and would make such a scandal out of this as should make his name stink from one end of London to the other. If he had any friends or any credit, we undertook that he should lose them. And all the time, as we were pitching it in red hot, we were keeping the women off him as best we could for they were as wild as harpies. I never saw a circle of such hateful faces; and there was the man in the middle, with a kind of black sneering coolness – frightened too, I could see that – but carrying it off, sir, really like Satan. 'If you choose to make capital out of this accident,' said he, 'I am naturally helpless. No gentleman but wishes to avoid a scene,' says he. 'Name your figure.' Well, we screwed him up to a hundred pounds for the child's family; he would have clearly liked to stick out; but there was something about the lot of us that meant mischief, and at last he struck. The next thing was to get the money; and where do you think he carried us but to that place with the door? – whipped out a key, went in, and presently came back with the matter of ten pounds in gold and a cheque for the balance on Coutts's, drawn payable to bearer and signed with a name that I can't mention, though it's one of the points of my story, but it was a name at least very well known and often printed. The figure was stiff; but the signature was good for more than that if it was only genuine. I took the liberty of pointing out to my gentleman that the whole business looked apocryphal, and that a man does not, in real life, walk into a cellar door at four in the morning and come out with another man's cheque for close upon a hundred pounds. But he was quite easy and sneering. '– Set your mind at rest,' says he, '– I will stay with you till the banks open and cash the cheque myself.' So we all set off, the doctor, and the child's father, and our friend and myself, and passed the rest of the night in my chambers; and next day, when we had breakfasted, went in a body to the bank. I gave in the cheque myself, and said I had every reason to believe it was a forgery. Not a bit of it. The cheque was genuine.'

'Tut-tut,' said Mr. Utterson.

'I see you feel as I do,' said Mr. Enfield. 'Yes, it's a bad story. For my man was a fellow that nobody could have to do with, a really damnable man; and the person that drew the cheque is the very pink of the proprieties, celebrated too, and (what makes it worse) one of your fellows who do what they call good. Black mail I suppose; an honest man paying through the nose for some of the capers of his youth. Black Mail House is what I call the place with the door, in consequence. Though even that, you know, is far from explaining all,' he added, and with the words fell into a vein of musing.

READERS CONNECT
WITH
VINTAGE CLASSICS

WILLIAM MAXWELL
THEY CAME LIKE SWALLOWS

This 1937 novel captures a brief time in the history of an American family living in an Illinois town in 1918, just at the end of the war. The story is remarkable for the way the book captures the view of

a child (remember it?) – that half-attentive, half-creative, essentially odd state of the eight-year-old, in which you tell yourself stories about how things work and how you belong to the world around you. For Bunny, his mother is the central element:

Instead of listening to the military terms of the armistice with Germany, Bunny went and put his head in his mother's lap, for he felt very odd inside of him. He heard her say, 'James, this child is burning up with fever!' and he thought dreamily that it must be so. I'm going to be sick, he thought, grateful for the cool hand on his forehead and her nearness. And after that, life was no longer uncertain or incomplete.

Through the eyes of first Bunny and then Robert, his thirteen-year-old brother, you are able to patch together the world of adult concerns. I really can't say much here without spoiling the story. It's the time of the great flu epidemic. The mother is pregnant. The father is patriotic and preoccupied. In Bunny's case we get our information because he eavesdrops; in Robert's case insight comes despite the boy's hearty lack of interest in grown-up matters. The boys' voices are beautifully distinct. The third and final section is told from the point of view of James, the father, so that formally the book takes the route of growing up. In three short steps we lose contact with childish things.

Lynne Hatwell (dovegreyreader) is a Devon-based community nurse

A child's world and voice of unfailing accuracy render this a novel of unerring depth and sadness with fear and wrong assumptions surrounding grief and loss. 'Little pitchers have big ears' and the reader has to listen carefully too, to intuit what it is the little fully-fledged mourners mustn't know. A book to read over and again.
* * * * *

Mette Steenberg is the founder/director of Laeseforeningen (The Reading Society) in Denmark

The first section told from the perspective of the young boy Bunny is probably the best piece of prose I have ever read! His sentiments become entangled with the environment, including his mother, to form a single unit which erases the distinction between inside and outside. This is child perception. In the final section packed with authentic, raw feeling, I surrendered wholeheartedly.
* * * *

Drummond Moir, once of Edinburgh, works for a London-based publisher

It's short and simple, but concentrated, utterly convincing and very moving. Maxwell's brilliant at conveying the gaps that exist even between family members who feel strongly about one another – Bunny's paranoia about his mother's affection; Robert feeling sorry after he tries to talk to his father at the same time that the father James knows they're 'of the same blood'. Poignant.
* * * *

STAR RATINGS

***** one of the best books I've read

**** one of the best I've read this year

*** highly recommended

** worth reading

* not for me but worth trying

0 don't bother

POETRY

SARAH LINDON

Strand

Starlings bank in unison:
a flock split and stretched,
its bonds twist and lengthen,
one flock, then three, then gone
on a graceful turn – and back
at once, substantial.

Beneath, surfers wait to rise,
to tack through twilight, crease
the water's skin and work
its cold salt flesh. We watch
as they patiently unfurl flight
from waves.

As day fails, pier lights start
and race, scatter bright design
against the night. I imagine you
light and strong as a hundred wings.
The birds become screaming
tumblers. Sea practises its reach.

THE POEMS OF MILLY JOURDAIN

Dawn Potter

As soon as I opened the flimsy paper cover of *Unfulfilment*, Joan Arden's tiny volume of poems, out fell the publisher's original review request: 'Mr Basil Blackwell has pleasure in submitting the accompanying book for review. He will be glad to receive a copy when it appears.' Clearly this was a message from the past that I needed to take seriously, especially since, as far as I can tell, no one else has ever reviewed this book. In fact, hardly anyone seems to have read it. Published in 1924, the collection appeared in the *Adventurers All* series, which Blackwell advertised rather poignantly as 'a series of young poets unknown to fame.' Several of these young poets did eventually become known to fame, including Dorothy L. Sayers, Aldous Huxley, and Sacheverell Sitwell. Joan Arden, however, did not.

The author's published name was a pseudonym. Her real name was Melicent Jourdain, known to her family as Milly; and I first came across Milly's poems as I was reading Hilary Spurling's 1984 biography of Ivy Compton-Burnett, whose longtime companion, Margaret Jourdain, was Milly's older sister. In addition to Margaret, an expert on furniture and the decorative arts, there were other fairly well known Jourdains in this large family: Philip, a mathematician and philosopher; Frank, a pioneering ornithologist; and Eleanor, who with a friend wrote a peculiar book in which they claimed to have seen the ghost of Marie Antoinette at Versailles.

Milly was the baby of the family and, like Philip, suffered from a hereditary disease known as Friedrich's ataxia, a rapidly advancing form of multiple sclerosis, characteristically revealing itself in childhood and killing its victims in their twenties. Both Milly and Philip managed to hang on longer than expected, but they were crippled for most of their lives. Philip was dead by age forty, while Milly lived slightly longer, dying at forty-four, which is, oddly enough, my own age as I write these words. To a degree, this coincidence accounts for my interest in her, but only as an afterthought. For as soon as I stumbled across the scraps of poems in Spurling's biography, I recognized that Milly was a real poet. Here, for instance, is 'Watching the Meet,' a poem that Spurling does not quote in her book but that struck me on first reading as a nearly perfect rendering of a fluid moment:

> The air is still so new and fresh and cold,
> It makes a warm excitement in our hearts
> To drive beside the sad and lonely fields.
> And now we see a wider space of road
> Where groups of horsemen moving restlessly
> Are waiting for the quiet-footed hounds.
> The hounds come swiftly, covering the way
> Like foaming water surging round our feet.
> And then with cries and sound of cracking whips
> All, all are gone: the distant beat of hoofs
> Like trailing smoke of dreams, comes fitfully
> To tell how near they were a moment past.
> But we see only winter trees again,
> And turning homewards meet a drifting rain.

Spurling had also recognized Milly's stature. *Unfulfilment*, she writes, 'records with singular terseness and clarity its author's decline into paralysis and death':

> The height of delight in Milly's poems is a single celandine or crocus in the grass, the feel of cold stream water, thin sunlight on glittering frost-covered hills. Perhaps she had learnt from Hardy or Wordsworth, perhaps simply from her own constricted life, the

deceptive simplicity that matches an unobtrusive verse form with an equally unassuming truthfulness. . . .

There is no way of dating Milly's poems. Some clearly gather intensity from being written in retrospect, after the Jourdains left Dorset in 1919, but all of them have a musicality, a concentration of thought and feeling, a desolate clarity.

Spurling's words are as close to a review of Milly's work as I can find. The book has more or less vanished from human memory; and when I did an internet search, only one copy seemed to be available anywhere for purchase. I bought it; and thus did Blackwell's review request come into my hands, tucked inside a frail forest-green volume, the cover so thin it might be construction paper, with title, author's name, and publisher's information printed on cream-colored paper and pasted austerely onto the green. The cheap, sad, scrapbook effect of the cover became even more noticeable once I caught sight of the glossy bookplate pasted inside; for, yes, someone else once owned this book: 'Arthur Melville Clark of Herriotshall and Oxton,' whose name reposes elegantly beneath a heraldic insignia topped with the fighting Scots motto 'blaw for blaw.'

Clark, at least career-wise, turns out to be less aggressive than his bookplate would indicate. He wrote several scholarly tomes, including studies of Sir Walter Scott and the playwright Thomas Heywood. In 1922 Blackwell published his *The Realistic Revolt in Modern Poetry*, and Clark is described on the title page as 'M.A. (Edin.)' and 'sometime lecturer in English at University College, Reading.' Perhaps Blackwell had entertained hopes that Clark would review Milly's book, but he doesn't appear to have done so. Nonetheless, someone, presumably Clark, read it, and his rare pencil marks in the margins can be illuminating, in a melancholy sort of way.

Style-wise at least, Clark's book on modern poetry is the usual sort of clotted, scholarly bombast. 'It is,' he declares, 'perhaps, unfair to emphasise the activities of the extremists – Messrs. Sassoon, Osbert Sitwell, T. S. Eliot, Edgar Lee Masters – but their very extravagance is instructive, as displaying in a greater degree the tendency more happily, if less obviously, illustrated by others.'

Whatever his statement might mean, it doesn't have much relevance to Milly Jourdain's poems, which are so distinctly unextravagant as to be nearly invisible to her book's marginal commentator. He marks only two poems in the collection. One is 'Watching the Meet,' where he pencils an unexplained X beside two lines. The other is 'The Leap over the Wall':

> **Now in my narrow room, my memory hears**
> **The waves break on the shore:**
> **I think of all the pleasant things behind**
> **That soon will be no more.**
>
> **I think of new-mown hay and summer days**
> **And slowly fading light**
> **And fields of white and shining snow that made**
> **Me breathless with delight.**
>
> **Of running water slipping through my hands**
> **And little pools most clear;**
> **Yet all these things have only made me sad**
> **And brought me close to fear.**
>
> **But could I rest at length on some great hill**
> **Watching the fading sky,**
> **Then I might know that peace above the earth's.**
> **And only wish to die.**

This is by no means the strongest poem in the collection. Jourdain is at her worst when she incorporates rhyme, at which point the poems tend to slip into a singsong periodically jolted by uneven meter. Nonetheless, even these lesser poems reveal her pure diction, her clear eye, and her strange and straightforward communion with sorrow, an honest hopelessness that she balances so eloquently with her love for life. But what the pencil jotter says is 'Morbid for no reason.'

On the whole, it seems we should be relieved that Clark never got around to reviewing *Unfulfilment*. Obscurity is a better fate than disdain, and Jourdain's poems are, at least superficially, easy to docket as old-fashioned poetess pieces about flowers and sheep and fog and sadness. Yet they bear, in their simplicity and their unflinching gaze, a resemblance to some of John Haines's tiny poems about the natural world. They are, as a friend said to me after reading a few excerpts, 'a figure in three dimensions.' And when Jourdain allows herself to relinquish her stultifying rhyme schemes, her lines blossom, becoming, as in 'The Floods Are Risen...,' deft and idiosyncratic statements on the link between external awareness and the inner life:

> **The great white sea has flooded all the land,**
> **And little waves are blown against the path**
> **With tiny sounds like dry and restless throbs:**
> **A white-sailed boat skims like a frightened moth**
> **Into the dusk: the grey clouds grow darker**
> **And dim the yellow light; we turn and leave**
> **The cold wind blowing on the ruffled sea.**

Occasionally she goes further: 'From a Road' layers unlineated stanzas of varying density to create a mélange in which the white space of the stanzas functions as the most delicate of line breaks:

> **Across the green valley the great hill raises its worn head through the pattern of fields which lie on its warm sides, brown in the summer sun.**
>
> **Above the line of dark green hedges, beech copses straggle to the top: rooks fly over it and little white clouds.**
>
> **The short grass is warm and the air is very clear.**
>
> **For a moment I think I am walking on the hill, stooping and touching the ground with my hands.**
>
> **But the trailing smell of honeysuckle from the hedge is blown to me, and I know that I cannot stir from the road.**

Unfulfilment was published two years before Milly's death in 1926. I don't know how many copies Blackwell printed or how many were sold. I don't know whether Milly paid for the printing herself. I don't know whether seeing her poems in print made her feel better or worse about the worth of her life and her imminent death. But the poems themselves... ah, they have not died.

ANTHONY TROLLOPE'S 'BEST NOVEL'

LADY ANNA

Suze Clarke

Brought up as an ordinary girl in the Keswick home of a Radical tailor, Thomas Thwaite and his son, Anna is also the disputed Lady Anna. Her mother, Countess Lovel, is altogether dependant on the tailor's charity, but determined to right the wrong done to her by Lord Lovel, the husband who told her while pregnant that he had another wife still living. (It becomes clear this was *most probably* a lie to free him from the burden of his new wife.) When, years later, Lovel dies, the young Earl, an unknown distant cousin, looks set to inherit and to unite the wealth and title of the family – until his lawyers discover that Anna and her mother have by far the stronger claim on the money, and that they are indeed the Countess Lovel and Lady Anna. It is decided by the lawyers that the best thing for both sides would be if the young people, Anna and the Earl, should stop being enemies and marry. The difficulty that gives shape to the novel is that Anna is already secretly engaged to Daniel Thwaite, the son of the tailor, and her only real friend from the impoverished early years.

Especially to modern eyes, it seems Anna is being sacrificed, urged to marry this unknown man for money and status. It is tempting to pre-conceive the Earl as a villain, a man without moral sense, and disorientating to discover that he is not mean or calculating. Anna sees with her first glance that:

He still had that sweet winsome boyishness of face which makes a girl feel that she need not fear a man,— that the man has something of her own weakness, and need not be treated as one who is wise, grand, or heroic. And she saw too in one glance how different he was from Daniel Thwaite, the man to whom she had absolutely given herself;—and she understood at the moment something of the charm of luxurious softness and aristocratic luxury.

She does not mean to accept the Earl and she does not fear him. If anything, she fears the man she really loves, as Trollope reveals in relaying the way Anna demurs at her attraction to the Earl: 'Had she been false-minded she had not courage to be false. But in truth she was not false-minded'. 'Truth', being true to Daniel, turns up in time to count, but it turns up after she has felt she lacks the courage to be false.

I find Trollope exhilaratingly useful. On one level, he is utterly clear about the nature of character and choice, on another, he is open about the impossibility of being clear even to oneself about one's own feelings. When left alone, Anna relives the meeting with her cousin, their kiss, and through it remembers Daniel's:

When her cousin touched her cheek with his lips she remembered that she had submitted to be kissed by one with whom her noble relative could hold no fellowship whatever. A feeling of degradation came upon her, as though by contact with this young man she was suddenly awakened to a sense of what her own rank demanded from her.

It's as if too much stuff – physical, social, moral, memory and present time – pushes to get expressed in just one language. The touch of her cousin's lips recalls the touch of another, and in response to that memory the 'feeling of degradation' is instantaneous and physical, like a blush, even though delayed or displaced. The degradation she feels is not at the contact with Daniel (though it goes back to him); it's the touch of the new lover, 'this young man', that 'awakens' the 'sense of what her own rank demanded from her'. But the socially conservative thought is felt with direct physical presence.

Trollope wrote in his *Autobiography* that '*Lady Anna* is the best novel I ever wrote!' Contemporary readers didn't share his enthusiasm and the book caused outrage when it appeared in 1874. Early on, just one-quarter through its serialisation in the *Fortnightly Review* – and while it was imaginably possible to influence the writer and the direction of the book – readers urged him to allow Anna to marry the Earl. Marriage to the journeyman tailor was unthinkable, as it is indeed to many of the characters in the book. After her engagement has become known, Anna pleads with her mother to remember how good Daniel had been to them in early days, to which the mother replies, 'If I praise my horse or my dog, do I say that they are of the same nature as myself?'

Trollope defers the meetings that electrify the book. You're a good way through before you see Anna and Daniel together, or can access Daniel's point of view. Trollope liked him, and meant to write a sequel to show what happens to Daniel later in life. He is a Radical like his father and a tailor too, only with him those instincts are supported by reading. He's a confirmed hater of privilege and rank who nevertheless means to give Anna the freedom to choose:

> **He cared nothing for the whole tribe of Lovels. If Lady Anna asked for release, she should be released. But not till she had heard his words. How scalding those words might be, how powerful to prevent the girl from really choosing her own fate, he did not know himself.**

In the world of whispered opinions and legal expedience, there's something big and operatic about Daniel's interventions that unite truth and feeling and purpose. But are they fair? Between the mother's plan deliberately to use 'the charm of luxurious softness and aristocratic luxury' to persuade Anna to fulfil her, the Countess's, ambitions, and Daniel's unknowingly strong words, the girl is caught in one of those great dilemmas that Trollope often makes central, where gradients of thought imperceptibly produce an absolute movement of mind.

BUCK'S QUIZ 48

FIFTY SHADES

Angela Macmillan

1. Who ignored the landlady's sexual advances in favour of her daughter?

2. Who (poetically) compared his wife in her nightgown to a skunk?

3. In which novel is the eponymous hero circumcised by a falling sash window?

4. Where did Lucy Honeychurch receive her first kiss?

5. In which novel do Swallow and Zapp unknowingly swap wives?

6. Who begged, 'Licence my roving hands and let them goe, / Before, behind, between, above, below'?

7. Who wrote, 'Here we are, without our clothes / One excited watering can, one peculiar rose...'?

8. Which angry couple reconciled their differences by becoming a squirrel and a bear?

9. Which writer won the Bad Sex Prize for Fiction for his novel about an affair between a retired bank manager and an 18-yr-old school-leaver?

10. Which novel centres on a prostitute who hates men and a wealthy perfume manufacturer?

11. What flowers complete the line: 'She stops to the sponge, and her swung breasts / Sway like full blown yellow...'?

12. What is the name of the fifteenth-century Arabic sex manual and work of erotic literature translated into English by Sir Richard Burton in 1886?

THE READER CROSSWORD

Cassandra

No.40

ACROSS

1. Become inflexible resulting in loss if you do (6)

*4. Riotous assembly of eaters for festival (6)

9. Inflammation found in nasty eye condition (4)

*10. Punish restraint (10)

*11 & 2 down. 27's oxymoronic poem about cold pudding? (6, 5)

12. Expected change left out (8)

13. Is he paler? Perhaps making him more attractive (9)

15. Is he in charge of stud? (4)

16. Musical often liberating when let down (4)

17. Relating to long-term plan about artist taking GCE (9)

21. This piece of music makes Poirot a romantic in retrospect (8)

*22. Lead in stirring up poetry of dissent (6)

*24. Act of atonement at the pawnbroker's maybe (10)

25. Said to be used by elevated speakers (4)

26. No accounting for these small quantities (4)

*27 & 16. Two Christian names for this poetic rector (6, 7)

DOWN

1. Outsize model wealthy but refusing to face facts (7)

*2. See 11 across

3. Senior journalist in wild sort of state (7)

5. A part each (6)

6. Call receiver (9)

7. These are almost identical when dead (7)

8. Ironic to see one hundred and fifty spinning particles of equal size (13)

14. It is absurd to lose every game (9)

*16. See 27 across

18. Leaders coming from a northerly direction all now turn east slowly (7)

19. For example I'm in a confused dream (7)

20. Three let rip boisterously (6)

23. Drain arranged in a new way at the lowest point (5)

* Clues with an asterisk have a common theme

116

PRIZES

The winner of the Crossword (plucked in time-honoured tradition from a hat) will receive a book prize courtesy of Vintage Classics, and the same to the winner of the fiendishly difficult Buck's Quiz.

Congratulations to Steve Bowkett of Cardiff and Tony Anstey of Birkenhead (Buck's Quiz), Steve Bowkett (Crossword).

Please send your solutions (marked Cassandra Crossword or Buck's Quiz) to The Reader Organisation, The Friary Centre, Bute Street, Liverpool, L5 3LA. The deadline for answers is 28 Jan, 2013.

ANSWERS

CASSANDRA CROSSWORD NO. 39

Across
9. Lifespan 10. Edict 11. Naive 12. Josephine 13. Sleuths 14. Aileron 17. Nodes 19. Tey 20. Grant 21. Soursop 22. Jutland 24. Schematic 26. Mafia 28. Cheer 29. Franchise

Down
1. Alan 2. Of time 3. Asbestosis 4. Banjos 5. Isostasy 6. Help 7. Miliaria 8. Stye 13. Sands 15. Legitimacy 16. Noted 18. Daughter 19. Tipstaff 22. Jackal 23. Affair 24. Sect 25. Mark 27. Abed

BUCK'S QUIZ NO. 47

1. Frank Churchill, *Emma* 2. Mr Laurence, *Little Women* 3. Jane Eyre 4. Sunday evenings, (D H Lawrence, 'The Piano') 5. *The Awakening*, Kate Chopin 6. Mr Jarndyce, *Bleak House* 7. Oscar Wilde 8. Wladislaw Szpilman 9. Edgar Drake (Daniel Mason, *The Piano Tuner*) 10. Henry James, *Portrait of A Lady*

ESSAY

REASON, AND LOSING IT

Alan Wall

Despite the well-known proverb to the contrary, one can surely not have too much of a good thing, so if reason is to be recommended, then how could one end up with a surfeit? Does not the phrase 'he has lost his reason' signify an unquestionable deprivation? Chesterton, sharply polemical as usual, says that 'he has lost his reason' is often literally preposterous, which is to say reversed: what the mad most often lose, he says, is all the other faculties. The reason alone remains, whirring away with a fearsome force, a motor of madness detached from all other considerations and requirements. Blake is not far from this in his notion of 'the spectre': this is a human being in whom the reasoning force has become entirely preponderant. Urizen represents the boundary that rationality always draws around the creative force. Energy is eternal delight. He who is left inhabiting the boundary that surrounded energy, once the energy itself has already departed, is spectral; all we have left now is the circumference of a centrifugal force whose power is no longer to be found within the magic circle.

And it is presumably in this Blakean sense that Brenda Maddox says of Yeats, being mocked as so often for his fascination with ghosts and spirits, that 'he preferred ridicule to an over-rationality like George Bernard Shaw's'. Over-rationality? The kind of spectre that should be avoided, then. Yeats once had a dream in which GBS was a sewing-machine, endlessly chattering away, but spewing out printed copy instead of cloth. So it appears that the rational faculty needs to be kept in balance with other affections and abilities. Swift's *Modest Proposal* shows what happens when rationality engages in its calculations without any check from human warmth and affection: you end by totting up the benefits that might accrue from eating the children of the poor. Reason is all right, it would appear, but only within reason. It should not declare itself a mighty god. If it does then, like Apollo, it will perpetrate acts of unspeakable cruelty, having Marsyas the satyr skinned alive merely for competing in music-making with the powers that be. The heart has reasons, Pascal reminded us, of which reason knows nothing.

Regan in *King Lear*, in stripping the old king down to his new place in the scheme of things, asks why he should have any followers at all: 'What need one?' Lear replies, with notable rationality: 'O! reason not the need'. This is a use we have lost: the idea of 'reasoning' as having things out between us, arguing the toss. This is handy-dandy, a word it is said Shakespeare took from John Florio's version of Montaigne, though he could presumably have just as well picked it up from Chapman's *Blind Beggar of Alexandria* of 1598, five years earlier. Handy-dandy, excessive two-handedness, being morally ambidextrous, represents a mode of which our greatest scholar is the Fool. The Shakespearian sense is more equivocal than our present one. If I reason with you now, then I am asserting my rectitude over your confusion. The sense of give-and-take, of profit and loss, is itself lost in the phrase 'I tried to reason with him', which really means: 'He is not merely wrong, but incorrigible in his mistakenness.' The Fool is only too aware that Lear is in the middle of a game of handy-dandy, where an object of value is hidden in one fist and you have to guess which one, as he ricochets between Regan and Goneril, trying to work out what modicum of retainers he might be permitted.

Edmund in the same play declares that his goddess is Nature, but he surely worships this newer version of reason too; a reason that can be seen in one light as a calculating machine, entirely unconstrained in its calculations by any custom or commandment, like Swift's proposer. Reason in its scheming, it would appear, may not always be as reasonable as one might wish. Something without rhyme or reason is presumably gratuitous, detached from expectation or resolution; it comes without the pleasure to be found in good verse, even good nonsense verse, and also without any seeming logic that might explain its teleology. By the third act of *Lear* we are out amongst the elements, with Mad Tom for company, and there's no longer any rhyme or reason to anything. Reason here, along with the traditional affections that might hold life together, has suffered ruination. But then Swift also quibbled over the notion that we are *rationalis*. *Rationalis capax*, he insisted. We *can* employ that faculty, but that doesn't mean we always do.

It was the burden of Adorno and Horkheimer's *Dialectic of Enlightenment* that reason itself, freed from other constraints, can become murderous. It is not merely the sleep of reason that breeds monsters, *pace* Goya; the Age of Reason can do so too. Voltaire's smile can lead on to Eichmann's book-keeping, since reason, in its affectless instrumentality, is capable of organizing genocide, notching up one more catalogue of demythologisation as it goes. What is there to stop it after all, if the *catalogue raisonnée* of a new belief system should so demand? Curiously, such a demonstration of reason's power appears in the end to be occluding reason itself. So we have the dreadful statement recorded by Primo Levi. On witnessing some outrage in the camps, the question was asked: 'Why?' '*Hier ist kein warum*' came the reply: Here there is no why. Amongst these utility buildings, reason has contrived to lose itself.

Reason is impeccably in the Romance mode, going back through the French to the Latin *rationem*. Mad is incorrigibly Anglo-Saxon, even though it might find a route etymologically all the way through to Sanskrit. Returning to Chesterton's remark, it could surely be the case that the word paranoid is misleading. The paranoid are not usually out of their minds – *para nous* – but locked altogether too firmly inside them. The terms for those 'not in their right minds' are often touchingly endearing.

Gazing on a world gone mad with the craze for versifying, Pope wrote: 'They rave, recite, and madden round the land.' His is the first recorded use of that word in the OED (initially in his version of *The Odyssey* in 1726), and it seems to me to be equally plausible transitively or intransitively. It never caught on, though maddening, its close relative, soon did. Such folk are, in varying degrees, bonkers, seemingly derived from the effects of a bonk on the head, and entirely unrelated to the tabloid usage 'bonk', meaning playful, exuberant, and occasionally well-rewarded sex. Currencies change, sadly, so tuppence short of a bob is now as useless idiomatically as 'bent as a nine-bob note', though 'a sandwich short of a picnic' still obtains. A favourite of my Yorkshire boyhood was' doolally-tap', variously spelt. I remember someone explaining to me at great length that the term came from the sound a piece of mill machinery made when one of its parts was malfunctioning, and this onomatopoeic reading still strikes me as plausible. However, the dictionaries record that it was actually derived from the Deolalie Sanatorium in Bombay, where deranged soldiers were sent, either to become underanged or to die. The tap part, it is speculated, might even take us to the Sanskrit *tapa*, meaning both heat and torment, all of which were presumably available in abundance, as long as you turned up at the right time of year.

CLIVE
SINCLAIR

FICTION

A BAD END

Clive Sinclair

Rabbi Goldfinch was a swine. About that, if nothing else, all his congregants agreed. Every shabbat, after the holy scroll had been returned to the Ark, he took his place on the bima and accused the worshippers of all manner of sins; of embezzelment, of fornication, of driving to the synagogue instead of walking. Nor was he hesitant about naming names. And yet there was never an empty seat in his synagogue. There was no mystery to this. What was the point of a rabbi who did not strike fear into the heart of a sinner? And who amongst them had clean hands and a spotless soul? Their God was quick to anger, and they expected no less of their rabbi.

His son, little Joshua, knew all about that. His lively ear, and uncanny cordination, made of him a musical prodigy. His father, the rabbi, did not deny him lessons with the émigré violinist who lived in the next street, but when it came to the matter of higher education, the rabbi lifted his flaming sword and barred the way. Instead Joshua was diverted to medical school, where he learned to play the veins and arteries, the muscles and sinews of the human body, as if they were so many violin strings.

After seven years it came to pass that the rabbi was able to boast, 'My son, the doctor.'

Needless to say, Joshua soon earned a reputation as a great
surgeon, a virtuoso of the operating theatre. But when the Angel
of Death tapped his father, the rabbi, on the shoulder, none of his
innumerable skills could save him. And so the rabbi, his father,
was buried by another rabbi in the traditional manner.

When Rabbi Goldfinch opened his eyes again it was not in
heaven, but in a pigsty.

'Oh my God,' he thought, 'the Buddhists were right. I have
been reincarnated as a pig.'

At first the idea of being devoured by gentiles filled him with
horror. But after a while he was able to console himself with the
consideration that – due to the laws of kashrut – he would never
be eaten by his own flesh and blood, and that his own son could
never become – albeit unwittingly – an incestuous cannibal.

After some days the rabbi began to suspect that his pigsty
was no ordinary pigsty. It was indoors, for one thing, and the
farmers all wore white coats, for another. And where was the
filth in which swine loved to wallow? On the contrary, this place
was spotless.

Meantime, the Angel of Death was abroad hunting new
quarry. He began to stalk an old fat man with a bushy white
beard. Although the man lived in the city he maintained a small
herd of reindeer. He fed them oats, but himself only mince pies
and port wine. With his X-ray eyes the Angel of Death was quick
to diagnose diabetes, which in turn was hastening end-stage
renal failure. The old man in the red dressing-gown was clinging
to life by a thread, even though he didn't yet know it.

But the Angel of Death, being eternally busy, had failed to
keep up with the latest developments in medical research: the
word 'zenotransplantation' was not yet in his lexicon.

In truth the technique was only in its rudimentary stage, and
Joshua, the rabbi's son, happened to be its chief practitioner.
When the word got out that Santa Claus was about to die for
want of a suitable kidney, he offered his services and those of
his experimental laboratory. The powers-that-be had no choice
but accept.

Back in the pigsty, the rabbi was beginning to enjoy his new
life. It was a huge relief not to be burdened with daily respon-

sibilities; no shaving, no sermons. Why he didn't even have to dress. Though he wasn't sure he would want anyone he knew to see him in such a state.

So it was with a mixture of joy and shame that he greeted the unexpected appearance of his own son. Both feelings squared then cubed when his son pointed to him, to him alone, and chose him from among the multitude.

How would his son greet him, the rabbi wondered as he was led along a neon-lit corridor, would he show the respect due to a father, even though that father was now a four-legged swine? The doors to his son's room were pushed apart and the rabbi gained entrance. But where was his son? All he could see was a bunch of masked men.

'Gonifs,' he thought, 'thieves.'

And he was right as usual, for they stole his kidney, and used it to restore life to Father Christmas.

As Joshua stared at the donor pig, still breathing on the operating table, the Angel of Death filled his ear with tempting words. He vouchsafed recipes known only in the Elysian Fields, and Joshua tasted the finished product on his tongue. If mere anticipation sent him into raptures, how could he resist the real thing?

When the operating theatre was empty, he cut the pig's throat with a scalpel, and butchered it expertly. He smuggled the joints into his deep freeze, which hitherto had known only kosher cuts. Although his family did not celebrate Christmas, they were sufficiently assimilated to exchange presents and eat the traditional fowl on December 25.

'My God, Joshua,' said his wife, who had never before tasted pork, 'that turkey was divine.'

CONTRIBUTORS

Patricia Canning is developing the Get Into Reading project across Northern Ireland and currently runs reading groups with female prisoners in Hydebank Wood, Belfast as well as with postgraduate Humanities students at Queen's University, Belfast.

Sue Charteris is a strategy consultant and leadership coach, and is Chair of Trustees of the Reader Organisation.

Emma Curran's poems have previously appeared in *Stand*, *The London Magazine* and *Poetry Wales*. She is currently researching a doctoral thesis on personification in women's poetry of the Romantic period.

Casi Dylan is Literary Learning Manager at The Reader Organisation, where she has worked since 2008. Born in Cwmystwyth, Ceredigion, she now lives in Glasgow although her work has taken her all over the UK as well as Denmark and Australia.

Seán Haldane is, by ancestry, something of a human compass: a quarter each English, German, Scottish and Irish. His poems are simply English. He has worked as a lecturer, part time farmer, small press publisher, psychotherapist, and consultant clinical neuropsychologist. He lives in London.

Chris Hardy's poems have appeared in numerous magazines, anthologies, (e.g. The Forward Prize) and websites. He has won prizes in the National Poetry Society's and other competitions. His third collection was published by Graft Poetry (www.graftpoetry.co.uk) in July 2012.

Iona Heath has worked as an inner city GP in Camden since 1975 (recently retired) and has just finished her term as President of the RCGP. She is internationally-known as a writer and speaker on the ethics and core values of general practice, contributing regularly to the *British Medical Journal*. She is the author of *The Mystery of General Practice* (1995) and *Matters of Life and Death* (2007).

Melissa Lee-Houghton's first poetry collection, *A Body Made of You* is published by Penned in the Margins. Her work has appeared in many magazines including *Magma*, *Poetry Salzburg Review* and *Tears in the Fence*. She is contributor to *The Silent History*.

Howard Jacobson was born in Manchester, educated at Stand Grammar School in Whitefield, and Downing College, Cambridge, where he studied under F. R. Leavis. His novels include *The Mighty Walzer* (winner of the Bollinger Everyman Wodehouse Prize), *Kalooki Nights* (longlisted for the Man Booker Prize) the Man Booker Prize-winning, *The Finkler Question* and, most recently, *Zoo Time* (2012).

Sarah Lindon's poems have appeared in *Magma, Poetry Wales, Seam* and *Stand,* and in *Tokens for the Foundlings* (Seren, 2012). She completed an MPhil in Writing at the University of Glamorgan this year.

Ian McMillan was born in 1956 and has been a freelance writer/performer /broadcaster since 1981. He presents *The Verb* on BBC Radio 3 every Friday night.

Alexis McNay is a project worker for Get Into Reading.

Andrew McNeillie's books include the memoir *An Aran Keening* (2001) and more recently In *Mortal Memory* (2010) and *Losers Keepers* (2011).

Dawn Potter directs the Frost Place Conference on Poetry and Teaching, held each summer at Robert Frost's home in Franconia, New Hampshire. Her latest book is an anthology, *A Poet's Sourcebook: Writings on Poetry, from the Ancient World to the Present,* forthcoming in early 2013.

Clive Sinclair's most recent book was *True Tales of the Wild West* (Picador 2008). His new collection of stories *Death & Texas,* of which 'A Bad End' is the conclusion, will be published next year.

Damian Taylor is Reader in Residence at Greater Manchester West Mental Health Trust.

Brian Turner served in the US army for seven years, including tours in Bosnia-Herzegovina and Iraq. His debut collection *Here, Bullet* (Bloodaxe Books) was awarded nine major literary awards; his second, *Phantom Noise,* was shortlisted for the 2010 T. S. Eliot Prize. He directs the low residency MFA at Sierra Nevada College.

Alan Wall is a novelist, short story writer, poet and essayist. His latest novel *Badmouth* will appear soon from Quartet Books. He is professor of Writing and Literature at the University of Chester.

Distribution Information

Trade orders Contact Mark Chilver, Magazine Department, Central Books

email: mark@centralbooks.com
web: www.centralbooks.com
tel: 0845 458 9925   fax: 0845 458 9912
Central Books, 99 Wallis Road, London, E9 5LN

All other queries regarding trade orders or institutional subscriptions
Contact The Reader Office

email: magazine@thereader.org.uk
tel: 0151 207 7207

SUBSCRIBE

the reader